MW01438601

EXERCISES

ON THE

ETYMOLOGY, SYNTAX, IDIOMS,

AND

SYNONYMS

OF THE

Spanish Language.

DESIGNED ESPECIALLY FOR SELF-INSTRUCTORS.

By L. J. A. M^cHENRY,

A NATIVE OF SPAIN,

Author of an " Improved Spanish Grammar," &c.

NEW EDITION, CORRECTED AND IMPROVED.

LONDON:
ARTHUR HALL, VIRTUE, AND CO.
25, PATERNOSTER ROW.
1852.

In the interest of creating a more extensive selection of rare historical book reprints, we have chosen to reproduce this title even though it may possibly have occasional imperfections such as missing and blurred pages, missing text, poor pictures, markings, dark backgrounds and other reproduction issues beyond our control. Because this work is culturally important, we have made it available as a part of our commitment to protecting, preserving and promoting the world's literature. Thank you for your understanding.

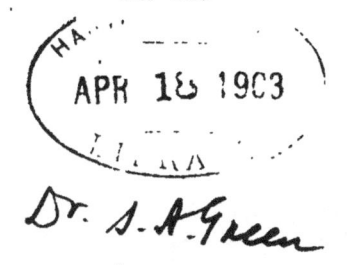

PREFACE.

The nature and object of Exercises on Grammar are too well understood, and their utility and importance, in elucidating or fixing, by practical application, the rules and principles of a language, too highly appreciated, to require any explanation, or to render much apology necessary for the introduction of the present volume.

That there are already in circulation several books of Spanish Exercises, some of them possessing considerable merit, the writer does not mean to deny; but he begs leave to observe that, as these have been adapted exclusively, or more particularly, to the different Grammars of their respective Authors, no work of this description existed, which, without much trouble and inconvenience, could be rendered subservient to the peculiar arrangement adopted in the Grammar lately published by the present Writer.

Thus circumstanced, and influenced by the many testimonies of approbation, both public and private, so liberally bestowed on his Spanish Grammar, of which several editions have been sold with unexpected rapidity, the Author felt anxious to prepare, with as much expedition as the pressure of business and due attention to the subject would permit, a suitable volume of appropriate Exercises. That such a work was really wanted he is much inclined to infer from the reiterated inquiries made for it, especially by those persons who have been pleased to give a preference to his former production.

Desirous of enhancing the utility of this little volume of Exercises, the Author has endeavoured to render them *progressively* difficult, partly by avoiding a repetition of the Spanish words, and partly by leaving undeclined every part of speech, which has already been, or which actually is, the immediate object of elucidation.

Having introduced Promiscuous or Recapitulatory Exercises, whenever it seemed necessary or expedient, the Author has ventured to deviate from the usual mode of concluding similar works, by substituting, instead of uninteresting or irrelevant extracts, a few Exercises on

iv   PREFACE.

the more common Idioms and Synonyms of the language; an innovation which he trusts cannot but prove greatly advantageous to every class of learners.

To conclude: the Author returns his sincere thanks for the liberal reception which his former work has experienced; and humbly trusts, that as, in composing this little volume, he has been invariably directed by the same desire as influenced him formerly,—that of facilitating the progress and promoting the improvement of the learner,—his present endeavours, however limited, will likewise receive some portion of that approbation so generally bestowed on every publication which has for its real object *the communication of knowledge.*

ADVERTISEMENT
TO
THE SIXTH EDITION.

The Author is duly sensible of the liberal encouragement with which the former Editions of these Exercises have been favoured, and confidently hopes that the several improvements which the present Edition has received will render the Work still more worthy of approbation. He has now published a

KEY TO THE EXERCISES,

which he trusts will facilitate the progress of the learner in acquiring a classical knowledge of the Spanish language, and thus furnish some additional claim to an extension of the public patronage.

EXERCISES
ON THE
ETYMOLOGY AND SYNTAX
OF THE
SPANISH LANGUAGE.

Preliminary Observation.

WHEN two or more English words are enclosed by brackets, the Spanish underneath is equivalent to the whole enclosure, and *vice versâ*. A horizontal line under the English implies a similarity of spelling, with this distinction, that a soft *t* in English must be changed into *c* in Spanish, and that the letter *s* is never to be doubled. Words having this mark ▲ underneath are not to be translated. Numerical figures preceding English words point out the Spanish arrangement. The letters *a, b, c,* &c. refer to the Notes in the Author's Grammar.

ON THE ARTICLE.

The Spanish articles are,

		Sing.	Plur.
	Masculine	el	los
The	Feminine	la	las
	Neuter	lo	

Agreement of the Article.

Rule 1. The article agrees in gender, number, and case, with the noun to which it is prefixed; as,

El *libro contenia* los *comentarios* de los *doctores* de la *universidad sobre* las *profecías* de los *profetas*.— *The* book contained *the* commentaries of *the* doctors of *the* university on *the* prophecies of *the* prophets.

The father was close to the mother; the sons behind
    padre estaba junto á   *madre*   *hijos detras de*
the daughters; the nephew before the niece; and the
  hijas   *sobrino delante de* *sobrina* *y*
sister between the brothers. The uncle sent by the
hermana entre   *hermanos.*   *tio mandó por*
husband the letter from the wife to the nieces, for
marido *carta* f. *de*   *muger*   *sobrinas, para*
the son of the aunt. The captains with the companies,
 hijo   *tia*   *capitanes con*   *compañias* f.
and without the general, marched towards the castle.
    sin   ———— *marcharon hacia* *castillo* m.
The intrepidity of the troops at the gates of the
  intrepidez f.   *tropas* f. *á* *puertas* f.
fortress excited the admiration of the colonels. The
fortaleza f. *excitó* ———— f.   *coroneles.*
angel announced the nativity to the shepherds in the
——m. *anunció*   *natividad* f.   *pastores en*
East.
oriente m.

Note a.—The eagle swam in the water of the pool.
       águila f. *nadó*   *água* f.   *laguna* f.
The waters of the sea drowned the birds. The boy
  águas   *mar* f. *ahogaron* *áves* f.   *muchacho*
broke the handles of the jugs and the handle of the
quebró *ásas* f.   *jarros* m.   *ása* f.
cup with the horn of the cow. The bird had lost
tasa f.   *ásta* f.   *vaca* f.   *áve* f. *habia perdido*
the tail and the wing in the trap.
  cola f.   *ála* f.   *trampa* f.

Note b.—The eagles of the army were deposited
      águilas   *exército* m. *fueron depositadas*

in the chapel of the college. The captain attributed
  capilla f. *colegio* m. *capitan* m. *atribuyó*
the victory to the assault of the castle, and not to
 victoria f. *asalto* m. *castillo* m. *no*
the hunger of the army. The wings of the bird
 hambre f.   *álas* *áve* f.
were clipped. The altar of the idol was behind the
estaban cortadas. *ara* f. *ídolo* m. *estaba*
altars of the goddess, and to the west of the temple.
aras *diosa*   *occidente* m. *templo* m.
The songster sang the air in the orchestra of the king.
 cantor m. *cantó* *ária* f. *orquesta* f. *rey*
The exploits of the warrior [obtained for him] the
 hazañas f. *guerrero* *le grangearon*
epithet of the Battler.
dictado m. *campeador.*

Promiscuous Exercises.

The affection of the mother was the cause of the
  cariño m.   *fué* *causa* f.
death of the sons. The ambassador received by the
muerte f.   *embaxador* *recibió*
courier of the queen, the letters from the minister of
correo m. *reyna* *cartas* f. *ministro*
the king to the emperor of the East. The culprit
 rey   *emperador*   *reo* m.
committed the crime close to the door of the gallery
 cometió *delito* m.   *puerta* f. *corredor* m.
of the house. In the beginning the Creator created the
 casa f.   *principio* m. *Criador creó*
heaven and the earth, divided the light from the dark-
cielo m. *tierra* f. *dividió* *luz* f. *tinie-*
ness, and made the firmament, and divided the waters
blas f. p.[*] *é hizo* *firmamento* m. *y*
which were [under] the firmament, from the waters
 que *estaban [debaxo de]*
which were above the firmament. The miracles of the
  sobre   *milagros* m.

[*] See Grammar, p. 77.

apostles were the proofs of the authenticity of the
apóstoles fueron   pruebas f.   *autenticidad* f.
mission. Abraham saw the ram entangled by the
mision f. *Abrahan vió   carnero* m. *enredado*
horns among the brambles in the mount. David
astas   entre   abrojos m.   *monte* m. ——
[played on] the harp.
   tocaba   arpa f.

Plural Number.

Rule 2. Nouns ending in a vowel which is not marked with the accent, take an *s* in the plural; as, *Reyno*, kingdom, *reynos*, kingdoms; *corona*, crown, *coronas*, crowns.

The sun, the moon, the planets, the stars, were the
   sol m.   *luna* f. *planeta* m. *estrella* f. *eran*
idols of the Egyptians. The Pagans sacrificed the
idolo m.   *Egipcio* m. *Pagano* m. *sacrificaban*
victims upon the altars of the idol. The planet Mer-
víctima f. *sobre*   Mercury is, of all the planets, the [nearest] to the sun.
curio es   todos   [*mas próximo*]

Rule 3. Nouns which end in an accented vowel, or in a consonant*, take *es* in the plural; as *Jabalí*, wild boar, *jabalíes*, wild boars; *árbol*, tree, *árboles*, trees; *luz*, light, *luces*, lights.

The thieves had scaled the walls of the gardens
   ladron m. *habian escalado   pared* f.   *jardin* m.
before the clocks of the churches had struck the
[*ántes que*]   *relox* m.   *iglesia* f. *hubiesen dado*
hour. The houses in the suburbs of the towns were
hora f.   *casa* f.   *arrabal* m.   *ciudad* f. *estaban*
full of the authors, who had written against the
llenas   *autor* m. *que habian escrito   contra*

* A final *z* must be changed into *c*.

authorities. The Peripatetics were the followers of the
autoridad f.   Peripatético m. eran   sequaz m.
philosopher Aristotle. The two farmers lived in two
filósofo m. Aristóteles   dos labrador vivian
rooms, which might, with greater propriety, be called
quarto m. que podian con mayor propriedad ser llamados
two   lofts   or lumberholes than apartments.
camaranchon m. ó zaquizamí m. que vivienda f.

Note a.—The oxen (2) had (1) not yet ploughed the
            buey m.   habian   no aun arado
fields, and numerous flocks of sheep were grazing
campo m. numerosas grey f. oveja f. estaban paciendo
in the verdant meadows. The kings and the emperors of
   verdes prado m.   rey   . emperador
the earth nominate judges who judge the transgressors
tierra f. nombran á juez m. que juzgan á transgresor m.
of the law [according to] the laws.
ley f. segun

Exceptions.—She acted only twelve Mondays, six
            ella representaba solo *   Lunes
Thursdays, and four Saturdays, in the year. Buy three
Juéves   Sábado   á   año m. compra
pen-knives and two gun-screws. The cook hung the
corta-plumas   sacatrapos   cocinero m. colgó
boiler   on the pot-hook, instead of putting it on the
marmita f. en llares f. en lugar poner la sobre
trevet. The stork drew with the beak the bone of
trébedes f. cigüeña f. sacó con pico m. hueso m.
the lamb from the gullet of the wolf. [Peruvian bark]
 cordero m. de fauces f.   lobo m.   la quina
often   cures the ague.
amenudo cura   tercianas f.

Promiscuous Exercises.

The acts of the parliament contain the laws of the
 ' acta f.   parlamento m. contienen

* See Cardinal Numbers, Grammar, page 37.

realm. The revolutions of the planets and the eclipses
reyno m.   *revolucion* f.   *eclipse* m.
of the sun are found   in the Ephemeris. The Ana-
         se encuentran   *efemérides* f.   *Ana-*
chorites in the deserts   are free from the effects of the
coreta m.   *desierto* m. *estan libres*   *efecto* m.
vexations of the world. The love of the subjects, and
vexacion f.   *mundo* m.   *amor* m.   *vasallo* m.
the efforts of the nations, are the succours of the kings
  esfuerzo m.   *nacion* f. *son*   *socorro* m.
of the earth, in the disturbances of the state. The
                      turbacion f.   *estado* m.
Israelites whom Moses delivered from the bondage of
Israelita m. *que · Moises*   *sacó*   *servidumbre* f.
the king of the Egyptians were six hundred thousand,
                          fueron seis cientos   *mil*
without counting the [old men,] the women, and the
  sin   *contar*   *anciano*   *muger*
children.
niño m.

Use of the Definite Article.

Henceforth the genders will not be marked, unless the nouns form exceptions to Rules 4, 5, and 6. See Grammar.

Rule 7. Nouns taken in a definite sense require the article; as—*Las virtudes de los santos*, the virtues of the saints.

The corruption of the heart is often the cause of
    corrupcion   *corazon es amenudo*   *causa*
the corruption of the mind. The printers   printed the
                      alma f.   *impresor imprimieron*
resolutions of the meeting in the gazettes of the govern-
resolucion   *junta*   *gazeta*   *gobi-*
ment. The death of the Saviour of the (2) human
erno   *muerte* f.   *Salvador*   *humano*

ON THE USE OF THE ARTICLE. 7

(1) race was announced to the world by the darkness
    género fué anunciada   *por*
which covered the face of the earth.
que cubrieron   *faz* f.

Rule 8. Nouns used in their most general sense are preceded by the article; as,—*La virtud es amable,* virtue is amiable.

Printers ought to know well   all the rules of ortho-
        deben A *saber bien todas   regla   orto-*
graphy. Death is a single moment between time and
grafía   *es un solo momento entre tiempo*
eternity. Pride and vanity are often the cause of
eternidad orgullo   vanidad son amenudo   causa
the misfortunes incident to (2) human (1) life. Interest,
    desgracia incidentes   humana   vida interes
glory, and ambition are commonly the motives of the
gloria   ———— *comunmente*   *motivo*
actions of men. Iron and steel are more useful than
accion hombre hierro acero   mas útiles que
gold and silver. The fear of the Lord is the beginning
oro   plata   temor   Señor es   principio
of wisdom.
sabiduria.

Rule 9. Names of empires, kingdoms, countries, provinces, mountains, rivers, winds, and seasons, generally take the article; as,—*La Inglaterra,* England; *el otoño,* autumn.

Ireland is more populous than Scotland. Europe,
Irlanda es mas populosa que Escocia   Europa
Asia, Africa, and America, are the four parts of the
Asia ———.   ———— *son quatro parte* f.
world. Olympus and Parnassus are famous mountains.
       Olimpo   Parnaso famosos monte
North, south, east, and west, are the cardinal winds.
norte sur este   oeste   cardinales viento

Spring, summer, autumn, and winter, are the four
primavera verano otoño hivierno
seasons of the year.
estacion

Note a.—England defended Spain against the attack
Inglaterra defendió á España contra ataque
of France. The eyes of Turkey watched the movements
Francia ojo Turquia observaban movimiento
of Russia. The Emperor of Germany set off from Russia
Rusia Alemania partió
in the spring, and spent the summer in Turkey. The
pasó
King of England [will go] to France.
irá

Note b.—Algiers is a kingdom of Africa. Tunis is
Argel es un reyno —— es
a (2) fertile (1) country. Genoa is a (2) maritime
fertil pais Génova marítimo
(1) country.

Note c.—The forty Martyrs of Japan are forty persons
quarenta mártir Japon persona
who suffered martyrdom in Japan. The greatest quan-
que padecieron el martírio mayor can-
tity of sugar and of rum, which [is consumed] in Eng-
tidad azucar ron que se consume
land, comes from Brazil.
viene ——

Rule 10 Nouns of measure, weight, &c., when preceded by the indefinite article in English, as an equivalent to *each*, require the article; as—*A veinte peniques la libra*, at twenty pence a pound; twice a month, *dos veces al mes*.

Wine [sells] at one dollar a bottle, butter at
vino se vende á un duro botella manteca
[eighteen] pence a pound, and eggs at twelve shillings
[*diez y ocho*] *penique libra huevo doce eschelin*

ON THE USE OF THE ARTICLE.

a hundred. The coffee, which the Egyptians buy at
ciento *café* *que* *compran*
four-pence a pound, [is sold] afterwards at two-pence
se vende despues dos
an ounce. My master comes twice a week, and
onza *mi maestro viene dos veces semana*
(2) charges (1) me twenty guineas a year.
carga me veinte ——— á el año

Note a.—The duties amount to ten crowns per bale.
derecho suben diez escudos por fardo
The courier received money [at the rate] of a shilling
correo recibió dinero á razon un
per mile.
milla

Note b.—Cut me a yard at four shillings and sixpence a
córtame vara quatro
yard, and ten yards at two shillings and a penny per yard.
diez

Rule 11. *Señor, señora, señorito, señorita,** when used in the third person of both numbers, require the article; as—*El señor Don Juan*, Mr. John. *Señora, dixo el Señor Don Rafael á su madre, no os acordais de haber visto esta cara?* Madam, said Mr. Raphael to his mother, do you not recollect having seen this face? N. B. *Caballero* follows the same rule.

[I have just learned], Mr. Gil Blas, that you are Mr.
acabo de saber que vm. es
Gil Blas of Santillana. Madam, said Mr. John Romero
——— *dixo Juan*
to Mrs. Gomez, I came to inquire how Miss Perez was.
vine á preguntar como estaba.
Messieurs Martinez and Company, [I am very sorry
compañía siento muchísimo

* See Grammar, p. 133.

to inform you] that Messieurs Garcia and Sons have
participarles á vms. *han*
failed. Gentlemen, is it possible that the gentlemen
quebrado *es* ᴀ ———
who have been here to-day (2) have (1) not inquired
que han estado aquí hoy hayan no preguntado
how the ladies were? [Young ladies], the [young
estaban Señorita
ladies] who were there yesterday [will not be] here
que estuvieron ahí ayer no estarán aquí
to-day.
hoy

Note *b*.—Doctor Harvey discovered the circulation of
——— *descubrió* ———.
the blood. Father Ysla translated the work of Mr. Le
sangre f. *padre traduxo obra*
Sage. King John granted many privileges to England.
Juan concedió muchos privilegio
Princess Amelia was the daughter of King George.
princesa ——— *era* ᴀ *hija Jorge*
Know then that I am the substitute of Doctor Sangrado.
sabete pues substituto Sangrado

Rule 12. Numerals, when denoting either the day of the month or the hour of the day, generally take the article; as—*El seis de Enero,* the sixth of January; *la una,* one o'clock; *las onze,* eleven o'clock; *las trez y quarto,* a quarter after three; *las ocho menos quarto,* a quarter to eight.

On the twenty-first of June the sun rises in England
ᴀ *Junio nace*
at a quarter before four, and it sets at a quarter pᴀ st
á se pone
eight. King George the Fourth was crowned on the
——— ᴀ *fué coronado*
19th of July, 1821, at one o'clock precisely. The
en punto

earthquake in the year one thousand seven hundred and
terremoto de   *año* ʌ   ʌ
fifty five, began at [about] a quarter before eleven in
        empezó á eso de   *de*
the morning of All Saints.
     día m.   *todo Santo.*

Rule 13. The article is generally repeated before every noun enumerated, especially when they differ in gender; as—*La Fé, la Esperanza, y la Caridad,* Faith, Hope, and Charity.

[I am not ignorant of] the virtue and wisdom of
    no ignoro   *virtud*   *sabiduria*
Ulysses. Where (2) wisdom (1) is, there is virtue,
         donde   *está ahí*
constancy, fortitude. Thus fell the (2) Roman (1) em-
constancia, fortaleza   *así cayó*   *Romano*   *im-*
pire, and involved in its ruins, fell likewise the arts
perio envueltas en sus ruinas cayeron tambien   *arte*f.
and sciences. Under the equator the days and nights
   ciencia debaxo de   *equador*   *dia* m.   *noche* f.
are equal. Patience and perseverance are necessary.
son iguales paciencia   *perseverancia*   *necesarias*

Rule 14. Two or more nouns, used in apposition, admit the article only before the first; as—*La ciudad de Londres, capital de Inglaterra, y residencia del soberano,* the city of London, the capital of England, and the residence of the sovereign.

Rule 15. Proper names of persons, places, and months, take no article; as—*Socrates,* Socrates; *Roma,* Rome; *Avril,* April.

Solomon the son of David was endowed with wisdom.
Salomon   —— *fué dotado de*
I am Telemachus, the son of Ulysses, the king of Ithaca.
yo soy Telemaco   ——   *Itaca*

ON THE USE OF THE ARTICLE.

[It would be very strange] that Rome, the sovereign
    seria bien de estrañar   *Roma*   *soberana*
and the mother of all the churches; that Rome, the
                   todas   *iglesia*   *que*
centre of truth and unity, [should teach] absurdities!
centro   *verdad*   *unidad*   *enseñase*   *absurdo*
Christian eloquence has for its object God himself, the
Cristiana eloqüencia tiene por su objeto á Dios mismo
source of all greatness.
orígen   *toda grandeza*
     Cicero and Quintilian divide style into three kinds.
     Ciceron   *Quintiliano dividen estilo en*   *género*
London and Paris are two famous capitals. July and
Londres   ——   *son*   *famosas capital*   *Julio*
August are the two   hottest   months in the year,
Agosto   [*mas calorosos*]   *mes de*
and December and January the two coldest.
     Diciembre   *Enero*   [*mas frios*]

     Note a.—Sunday is a day which we ought to
               Domingo   *un dia*   *que*   ▲ *debemos* ▲
consecrate to God. Ash Wednesday is the first day of
consagrar   *Miércoles de ceniza es*   *primer*
Lent. [He will return] Friday or Saturday.
quaresma   *volverá*   *Viérnes ó Sábado*

     Note c.—The (2) unpleasant (1) adventure which
                     pesado   *lance*   *que*
I had had in the house of the grocer. The innkeeper
habia tenido en   *especiero*   *mesonero*
(2) conducted (1) me to the house of a carrier.
    conduxo   *me*   *un arriero*
[Ye know not] what men [ye have] in the house.
vosotros no sabeis que   *teneis*

     Note d.—[It is better] to be loved with respect than
             mas vale   ▲ *ser amado*   *respeto que*
with tenderness. Libertines live without faith and with-
    ternura   *libertino viven sin*   *fé*

ON THE USE OF THE ARTICLE. 13

out religion. We ought to suffer with patience the
———— debemos ▲ sufrir paciencia
inconveniences of this life.
incomodidad esta vida

Rule 16. Nouns, taken in a partitive sense, are never preceded by the article; as—*Dame pan,* give me bread; *dale vino,* give him some wine; *danos miel,* give us honey.

New kings, new laws. Besides gold and silver,
nuevos nuevas ademas de oro plata
Europe draws from the New World pepper, sugar,
saca nuevo pimienta azucar
tobacco, and several other things. I reserve my rooms,
tabaco varias otras cosa reservo mis quarto
said the landlady, for people who [do not sup on] bread
dixo mesonera para gente que no cenan
and cheese. The world abounds in snares, difficulties,
queso abunda lazo dificultad
and dangers. [There are] authors in whose writings
peligro hay cuyos escrito
[we discover] more rhetoric than eloquence.
descubrimos mus retórica que elocuencia

Note a.—Without reckoning some rials more, which
contar real que
[I had stolen from my uncle.] I have some idea of
habia hurtado á mi tio tengo
having seen that face. Men [are ashamed] on some
haber visto esa cara se avergüenzan en
occasions of their best actions.
ocasion sus mejores accion

Note b.—[Has the post brought] any gazettes?
ha traido el correo
[It has not brought] either gazettes or journals.
no ha traido ni ni diario
[Are there] any pens in the inkstand? [Is there] any
hay pluma tintero hay
wine in the bottles?

14 NOUNS.

Note c.—Send me some water in a glass. The
   Mándame ▲   *un vaso*
doctor attributed the indisposition to some [roast meat]
  atribuyó   ——————   *asado*
which he had eaten. [It is requisite] to rub the
que *habia comido* *es menester* ▲ *frotar*
bruises with some vinegar.
cardenal   *vinagre*

Note d.—Charles the Second, son of Philip the Fourth,
   Carlos segundo   *Felipe quarto*
left the crown to Philip the Fifth. William the Third
dexó *corona*   *quinto Guillermo tercero*
married Princess Mary, daughter of James the Second,
casó con princesa Maria *hija*   *Jaime*
and grand-daughter of Charles the First. Volume the
  nieta   *primero*
ninth, chapter the thirteenth.

Note e.—I bought yesterday a book entitled, The
   compré ayer un libro intitulado
Letters of Clement the Fourteenth. The life of
carta *Clemente* *catorce*
Cervantes [is found] at the beginning of his best work,
—————— *se halla á*   *su mejor obra*
entitled, The Life of Don Quixote. Mr. Capmany has
intitulada   —————— *señor* —————— *ha*
written an excellent work on the philosophy of elo-
escrito una excelente *sobre* *filosofia elo-*
quence, entitled The philosophy of eloquence. We have
cuencia intitulada   *hemos*
read the life of Don Quixote.
leido ——————

NOUNS.

Rule 17. When two nouns, signifying different things, come together in English, their order is reversed in Spanish, and the preposition *de* prefixed to the second; as—Man's nature, *La naturaleza del hombre;* marble pillar, *Columna de mármol.*

Diana's anger was the cause of Acteon's death, and
Diana cólera fué ———
Helen's beauty of Troy's destruction. Wisdom's pre-
Elena hermosura Troya destruccion pre-
cepts form man's heart. The king of England's [eldest
cepto forman primo-
son] is Prince of Wales. The gospel is the Christian's
génito es príncipe Gales evangelio es Cristiano
rule. Nature's gifts are for man's advantage.
regla naturaleza don son para ventaja
[There are] many silk-worms in Italy. Battles were
hay muchos seda gusano Italia batalla eran
more bloody before the invention of fire-arms.
mas sangrientas ántes de ——— fuego arma
King Sesostris was seated on an ivory throne.
——— *estaba sentado en un marfil trono*
Easter Sunday is the last day of Lent. [Let not thy
Pascuas Domingo es último dia quaresma que no sean
promises be] like court promises.
tus promesas como corte

Note a.—The ten commandments were written upon
diez mandamiento estaban escritos sobre
two tables of stone. (2) Sensual (1) pleasures are
tabla piedra sensuales placer son
enemies to reason and to virtue. The (2) second
enemigo razon f. *dos*
(1) chapter treats of the frights which he had in the
capítulo trata susto que tuvo
road to Peñaflor; and the ninth of the journey of Scipio
camino ——— nueve viage Scipion
to Madrid, and his return to Segovia.
su vuelta ———

Note b.—Claudina acknowledged to her sister that
——— *confesó su hermana que*

16 NOUNS.

the rogue of a Moor (2) had (3) deceived (1) her.
pícaro el Moro habia engañado la

Note c.—A clerk of the merchant's delivered the
uno dependiente comerciante entregó
memorial to a page of the prince's. [We walked] in
uno nos paseamos en
the queen's garden, and then went to see a garden
reyna luego fuimos á ver uno
of the emperor's.

Note e.—Go to the surgeon's. [I went into] the
ve cirujano entré en
first notary's. [Going out] of the pastry-cook's.
primer escribano al salir pastelero
[He took refuge] at the governor's.
se refugió en

Promiscuous Exercises.

Among the Egyptians the lion was an emblem of
entre leon era a símbolo
vigilance. Ignorance is one of the consequences of the
vigilancia ignorancia es una conseqüencia
corruption of nature. Justice and clemency are the
naturaleza justicia clemencia son
support of thrones. Lot retired to the borders of Jordan.
apoyo — se retiró orilla
In Turkey the scimitar is the interpreter of the Koran.
cimitarra es intérprete alcoran
History, geography, and mathematics, are (2) necessary
historia geografía matemática son necesarias
(1) sciences. [Let us be] frugal without covetousness,
seamos frugales avaricia
and liberal with moderation. [Let us accompany him] to
liberales acompañemosle a
Calvary. Haughtiness, presumption, and deceit, commonly
Calvario altivez f. presuncion engaño de ordinario
eat and sleep with riches. [We paid] the coachman
comen duermen riqueza pagamos cochero

NOUNS.

[at the rate] of tenpence a mile. Señora Leonarda,
á razon   *milla*
said one of the horsemen, [look at] this [young man].
dixo uno   *caballero*   *mire*   *este*   *mozito*
[Let us prefer] virtue to interest. Pythagoras taught
prefiramos   *interes*   *Pitagoras enseñó*
the immortality of the soul. Painters express with
inmortalidad   *alma*   *pintor expresan*
colours the passions, which poets express with
color   *pasion*   *que*   *poeta* m.
words. Señora Leonarda served the nectar to those
voz   *servia*   ———   *aquellos*
(2) infernal (1) gods. The mines of Peru produce
infernales   *mina*   ——*producen*
gold, silver, and diamonds. We heard some voices in
diamante   *oimos*
the street. Man's life is full of troubles. Sovereigns
calle f.   *vida está llena*   *trabajo*   *soberano*
[seldom] read the truth, unless when they read the
rara vez   *leen*   *verdad sino quando* A
maxims of the Gospel, or the axioms of Euclid. Charles
máxima   *evangelio* ó   *axioma* m.   *Euclides*
the Fourth's abdication took place in the eyes of France.
           ——— *tuvo efecto á*
King William and Queen Mary ascended the throne of
                          subieron á
England on the thirteenth of February, one thousand
           A   *Febrero*   A   *mil*
six hundred and eighty-nine. The king of England
seis cientos   A
sent an ambassador to the Emperor of China. Prudence,
envió un embaxador   *prudencia,*
justice, fortitude, and temperance, are the four (2)
justicia, fortaleza,   *templanza*   *son*   *quatro*
cardinal (1) virtues. Injuries and affronts are the
cardinales   *injuria*   *afrenta son*
keys to the heart. Hypocrites are objects of God's
llave f   *hypocrita*   *son*   *objeto*

hatred, and of men's indignation. The road to
aborrecimiento camino
heaven is full of thorns. Abraham obeyed the Lord's
cielo está lleno abrojo Abrahan obedeció á
voice. [Behold] that man who has been your shield
aquí teneis á aquel que ha sido vuestro escudo
in war and in peace, the honour of nature, and the
guerra paz f. honra naturaleza
glory of the (2) Roman (1) nation. We experienced
gloria Romana experimentamos
the same terror which we had inspired in the house
mismo que habiamos inspirado
of Camilla.

OF ADJECTIVES.
Their Feminine Termination.

Rule 18. Adjectives which end in *o*, *an*, or *on*, have their feminine termination in *a*. Those terminating otherwise are common to both genders; as—
El muchacho holgazan, the idle boy; *la muchacha holgazana,* the idle girl; *el dia feliz,* the happy day; *la hora feliz,* the happy hour

The mistress was sly and the maid idle. The
ama era socarron criada haragan.
life everlasting is desirable. The death of the [righteous
perdurable es apetecible justo
man] is a happy death. Experience is fatal to many.
es una feliz experiencia es muchos
The grace of God is efficacious. Charity is a (2) humble
gracia es eficaz es una humilde
(1) virtue.

Note a.—The hour of death is uncertain. Nature
hora es incierto
never is unemployed. The victory obtained by Cæsar
nunca está ocioso victoria conseguida por——

in the plains of Pharsalia was baneful to his country,
llanada Farsalia fué destructivo su patria.
pernicious to the Romans, and dismal to human nature.
pernicioso Romano funesto humano

Note b.—(2) Scotch (1) music is soft and harmo-
Escoces música es suave armo-
nious. The fandango is a (2) Spanish (1) dance.
nioso ——— es una Español danza
[Bull-feasts] are an (2) Andalusian (1) diversion. Her
fiestas de toros son una Andaluz ——— su
Saxon Majesty came in a (2) Danish (1) vessel.
Saxon magestad vino una Dinamarques embarcacion.

Note c.—The English cloths are woven with a
Inglaterra paño estan texidos una
mixture of Spanish wool. The ship's cargo consisted
mezcla España lana navio cargazon f. consistia
of Dutch cheese, Italian silk, Portuguese wine, Ame-
en Olanda queso Italia Portugal Amé-
rican wheat and Russian tallow.
rica trigo Rusia sebo.

Note d.—The Turkish ambassador dined yesterday
comió ayer
with the Russian consul, and the American plenipo-
plenipo-
tentiary.
tenciario.

Plural of Adjectives.

Rule 19. The plural of adjectives is formed like the plural of substantives; as—*santo, santos, Saxon, Saxones, Andaluz, Andaluces.* See Rules 2 and 3.

Place of Adjectives.

Rule 20. Adjectives, and participles used adjectively, are generally placed after their nouns; as—*Operaciones difíciles,* difficult operations; *gene-*

20   OF ADJECTIVES.

rales vencidos, conquered generals; *soldados heridos,* wounded soldiers.

Agreement of Adjectives.

Rule 21. An adjective agrees with its noun in gender, number and case; as—*Argumento ridículo,* ridiculous argument; *conclusiones falsas,* false conclusions.

Exception. Adjectives are always put in the masculine when they qualify the noun *nada.* See Grammar, p. 97.

The recollection of the virtuous actions of illustrious
    memoria   *virtuoso* ——   *ilustre*
men excites our veneration.
varon excita ———

The Divine perfections are interesting to man. Igno-
   Divino perfeccion son interesante   *igno-*
rant men are generally obstinate. Delicious viands
rante son generalmente pertinaz delicioso vianda
are poisoned pleasures. Premature [old age] is the
son emponzoñado gusto   anticipado vejez f. *es* a
fruit of a luxurious life.
fruto una luxurioso

A sublime style does not consist in a diction loaded
un ——— *estilo* a *consiste una diccion cargado*
with useless epithets, pompous phrases, and high-sounding
de ocioso epiteto pomposo frase f. *alti-sonante*
words. [At the end] of five or six years I understood
palabra al cabo   *entendia*
a little the Greek authors, and [sufficiently well] the
un poco Griego   suficientemente
Latin poets. Nothing is so impetuous as the desires
Latino poeta   es tan impetuoso   deseo
of self-love, nor so secret as its designs.
amorpropio ni secreto sus designio.

Note a.—The author refutes the artful objections
                  refuta   *artificioso objeccion*

OF ADJECTIVES.

of his sophistical antagonists, and [endeavours to]
   sus sofístico antagonista m.   *se empeña en*
dispel   the ridiculous doubts of pusillanimous believers.
desvanecer   ridículo duda   pusilánime creyente
The experienced pilot perceived [from afar] the
   experimentado piloto percibió   de lejos
towering summits of the mountains of Leucata. The
empinado cima   monte
mild zephyrs, more powerful than the burning beams
dulce zéfiro mas poderoso que   ardiente rayo
of the sun, preserved a grateful coolness. An expe-
         conservaban grato frescura un
rienced pilot foresees danger. A [very happy] death is
         preve peligro   dichosísimo   es
the fruit of a very pious life.
        piadosísimo

Note b.—The bride was so ugly that it gave little
        nóvia era tan feo que a *daba poco*
pleasure [to look at her.] Ambition augments the many
gusto el mirarla   ambicion aumenta   mucho
troubles and · lessens the few pleasures, which [are
pena   disminuye poco placer   que   se
found] in the world.
hallan

Note c.— [I met]   sometimes with certain Scotch
    encontrábame alguno vez f.   *cierto Escoces*
students. [He approached me] with a certain cheerful
estudiante   acercóse á mí   a   alegre
and hasty air. The silence and obstinacy of the
apresurado ayre   silencio obstinacion
criminal were evident proofs of the crime.
reo eran cierto prueba   delito

Note d.—Of two evils [we ought] to choose the least.
        mal debemos a *elegir menor*
The lunar cycle is a period of nineteen solar years, or
  lunar ciclo es un periodo   solar año ó
of nineteen lunar years and seven intercalary months.
                          intercalar mes

The forty-second chapter contains forty-two paragraphs.
         capítulo contiene   *párrafo*

Note e.—The goddess and the nymphs held their eyes
         diosa   *ninfa tenian los ojo*
fixed on the young Telemachus, so interesting (2) was
fixo en   *interesante*   *era*
to (1) them his history. The pleasures of life are very
A   *les su historia*   *placer*   *son muy*
few. How certain were her suspicions! When the
    quan cierto fueron sus sospecha   *quando*
laws are many [they occasion] confusion.
son   *causan*   *confusion.*

Note f.—Self-love is the greatest of all flatterers.
                  es   *mayor*   *todo adulador*
God is the creator of all things. Charity is the greatest
es criador   *cosa*   *caridad es*
of all Christian virtues. Ingratitude is the greatest of all
    Cristiana   *ingratitud*
vices. All happiness is a gift of the (2) divine
vicio   *dicha*   *es un don*   *divino*
(1) hand. All the [reward he merits] is not great.
mano f.   *recompensa que merece es*   *grande.*

Rule 22. Two or more nouns in the singular require their adjective in the plural; and in the masculine termination if they differ in gender;—as *El palacio y el templo magníficos,* the magnificent palace and temple: *la iglesia y el hospital edificados por él,* the church and hospital erected by him.

The love of life and the fear of death are natural
    amor   *temor*   *son natural*
to men. Pride and misery come frequently united.
    orgullo miséria vienen freqüentemente junto
Health and power are uncertain and perishable; but
salud poder son incierto perecedero pero

OF ADJECTIVES. 23

glory and virtue are certain, solid, and durable. The
gloria   son cierto sólido
husband and wife buried; the son and daughter ill;
marido   muger enterrado   hijo   hija enfermo
and the aunt and niece [given over]: this was the sad
          tia   sobrina desauciado   esta era   triste
condition of that unhappy family.
          aquella desdichado

Note *a*.—The wonderful prudence and judgment
              maravilloso prudencia   tino
manifested in the last battle. The supreme power and
manifestado último batalla   supremo poder
authority with which he governs.
autoridad   que él gobierna

Rule 23. An adjective agrees with the *nearest* of two or more plural nouns, which differ in gender, as—*los efectos y las riquezas preciosas, las riquezas y efectos preciosos*, the invaluable riches and effects.

The knowledge of (8) political (1) frauds and
         conocimiento   político   fraude
(2) connivances is necessary [to him that governs]. The
    connivencia es   al que gobierna
army consisted of conscripts from the (3) Italian (1) re-
exército consistia en conscripto   Italiano   re-
publics and (2) estates. The mistaken philosopher [had
pública   estado   engañado   filósofo   re-
recourse] to (3) ridiculous (1) arguments and (2)
curria   ridículo   argumento
objections. The many assemblies and conventicles
objeccion   asamblea   conventículo
alarmed the Gallican church.
asustaron á Galicano iglesia.

Note *b*.—His Majesty was resolved; but [has been]
          su Majestad estaba resuelto pero se ha visto
compelled to abandon the project. His Holiness has
precisado á abandonar proyecto   Santidad ha

OF ADJECTIVES.

been deprived of his friends, and his Highness is
sido privado   sus   amigo   Alteza esta
banished. His Excellency has been pleased to grant
desterrado   Excelencia ha sido servido de conceder
that their Lordships be buried in the Chapel Royal.
que sus Señoria sean enterrado   real

Note c.—Then the widows [saw themselves] aban-
          entonces   viuda   se vieron   aban-
doned, and the orphans [found themselves] unpro-
donado   huérfano   se hallaron   desam-
tected; the Romans being then no more than the
parado   siendo   no mas   que
shadow of themselves. Self-love makes man an idolater
sombra   si mismo   hace á   a idólatra
of himself.
sí mismo.

Observation.—The arrival of the (2) French and
                llegada   Frances
(3) Russian (1) commissioners has given rise to many
    Ruso   comisionado   ha dado origen
rumours. The Iliad and the Eneid are the pictures of
rumor   Iliada   Eneida son   pintura
the (2) Greek and (3) Roman (1) nations.

Rule 24. *Primero, tercero, postrero, uno, alguno, ninguno, bueno,* and *malo,* lose (when prefixed) the *o* in the singular; as, *el primer hombre,* the first man; *el postrer dia,* the last day; *ningun juez,* no judge; *un buen poeta,* a good poet; *un mal lector,* a bad reader; *una mala vida,* a bad life.

Troubles and afflictions are the inheritance which
    pena   afliccion   son   herencia   que
our first parent (2) left (1) us. Hope (2) con-
nuestro primero padre   dexó   nos   esperanza con-
ducts (1) us to the end of life through an agreeable
duce   fin   vida   por uno agradable
road. The first of God's commandments is that
camino   mandamiento es que

OF ADJECTIVES. 25

[we should love him]. For thy journey [I will give
    le amemos   *para tu viage*   *te daré*
thee] some money. Laws are useless in a bad
    alguno dinero   *ley son inútil*   *uno malo*
government.
gobierno

Note *a.*—[He rose again] on the third day [according
        resucitó ▲   *tercero*   *segun*
to] the scriptures. William the Third was the third king
   escritura   *fué*
of England after the Commonwealth.
      despues de   *república.*

Note *b.*—[They all agreed that I was worth] a
        convinieron todos en que valia ▲
hundred times more than my predecessor. They lost
ciento vez mas que mi predecesor   *perdieron*
a hundred frigates, and one ship of a hundred and twelve
▲   *fregata*   *uno navio* ▲   *doce*
guns.
cañon.

Note *c.*—Saint Paul is called the Apostle of the
    Santo Pablo es llamado   *Apóstol*
Gentiles. The bridegroom lived in the parish of Saint
Gentil   *nóvio vivia*   *parroquia*
George, and the bride in that of St. Mary, but [they
Jorge   *nóvia*   *la*   *pero*
were married] in the church of St. Dominic in the parish
se casaron   *Domingo*
of St. Thomas.
    Tomas

Note *d.*—I manifested a great desire to [accompany
        mostré ▲ *grande deseo de acompañar*
them]. [There was] a great entertainment. His great
los   *hubo uno*   *convite*   *su*
anxiety was caused by his great love. In this manner
ansia era causado por   *amor de esta manera*

I obtained a great reputation [for wisdom] in all the
   logré   *fama*   *de sábio*
city.
ciudad.

   Note e.—A friend never can [be discovered] in prospe-
        amigo nunca puede descubrirse *prospe-*
rity, nor an enemy concealed in adversity. [He carried
ridad ni   *enemigo ocultarse* *adversidad* *llevóme*
me] to a cellar, where I saw an infinity of bottles.
    bodega donde *vi* *infinidad botellas*

   Note f.—The dangerous state of the patient did not
          peligroso   *enfermo* ▲
allow any delay. [You run not] any risk, (2) said
permitia tardanza *no correis* *riesgo* *dixo*
(3) he to (1) them. [There is no] law so violated as
  él ▲   *les*   *no hay*   *tan violado como*
that which (2) commands (1) us to forgive injuries.
la que   *enseña*   *nos á perdonar*
We saw no living object in those mountains.
vimos *viviente objeto* *aquellos montes.*

   Rule 25. Adjectives, or participles employed as substantives, require the neuter article, if such words as *how, how much, what,* or *that which,* can be prefixed to the English adjective, and in other instances take the masculine or feminine article agreeing with the noun understood; as,—*Los jóvenes no conocen bien lo ventajoso que les será prepararse para lo futuro,* The young do not well know how advantageous it will be to them to prepare themselves for the future; *Muchas son las penas verdaderas, pero las imaginarias son mas,* Many are the real troubles, but the imaginary ones are more.

   Youth (2) has (1) not foresight of the future,
juventud   *tiene*   *no prevision*   *futuro*
experience of the past nor moderation to [conduct
experiencia   *pasado ni* ———— *para condu-*

OF ADJECTIVES.

itself] in the present. If God tolerates the unbelieving
cirse   presente   si   tolera   incrédulo
we ought to suffer them. The ambitious sacrifice
nosotros debemos ʌ *sufrir los   ambicioso sacrificar*
[every thing] to fortune. Longinus wrote on the
    todo   fortuna   Longino escribió sobre
sublime. The idle are useless to society. The
                perezoso son   inútil   sociedad
marvellous always surprises. The Catholic religion
maravilloso siempre sorprende   Católico
(2) is (1) not like the [false ones] which consist in
es   no como .   falso   que consisten
an exterior worship. We ought always to have pre-
      culto   debemos siempre ʌ *tener pre-*
sent how important it is to employ well our time,
sente importante que es ʌ *emplear   nuestro tiempo*
and how uncertain it is that we (2) [shall enjoy] (1) it
     incierto   que ʌ   *disfrutarémos   le*
to-morrow.
mañana

On the use of the numeral adjective *uno*, as a substitute for the English indefinite article, see Observation, Grammar, page 100.

1. Fortune is a capricious deity. Calypso saw a
    es   caprichoso deidad   vió
rudder and a mast, the remnants of a vessel which
timon   mastil   resto   navio que
[had just been wrecked]. [He that] loses a friend loses
acababa de naufragar   quien pierde amigo
a defender.
defensor

2. A solitary life (2) has (1) no attractions for an am-
   solitária   tiene   no atractivo para
bitious man. A (2) good (1) man never can be mise-
                             nunca puede ser desdi-
rable, nor a (2) wicked (1) man happy. A man without
chado   malo   dichoso

OF ADJECTIVES.

virtue (2) envies (1) it in others. An obedient wife
   envidia la otros   obediente
commands her husband.
manda á su

 4. Apelles was a painter, Cicero an orator, and Virgil
   Apeles era pintor   orador Virgilio
a poet. An astronomer or an anatomist (2) can (1) not
    astrónomo anatómico puede no
be an atheist.
ser ateista

 5. The best coffee comes from Mocha, a town of Arabia
   mejor café viene ——— ciudad ———
Felix. Newton, an English philosopher, was buried in
Dichoso ———   fué
Westminster Abbey, an honour granted to few.
———————— abadia honra concedido poco

 6. At last, after having eaten and drunk, he wished
  en fin despues de haber comido bebido á quiso
to put an end to the farce. We made a beginning to
á poner fin comédia á dimos principio
a long conversation. I have not had an opportunity
 largo ———— á he no tenido ocasion
of [speaking to him]. [Do not make] a noise. Have
  hablarle   no hagas ruido ten
a care.
cuidado

 7. A treatise on the longitude. An exposition of
   tratado   longitud.   ————
the Christian doctrine. A sketch of the manners of the
 Cristiano doctrina bosquejo costumbre f.
Indians.
Indio

 8. Cleopatra had two pearls, and each [was worth]
  ———— tenia perla cada una valia
a million. Argus had a hundred eyes. No man ever
 millon Argo   ninguno jamas

OF ADJECTIVES. 29

lived a thousand years. The city of Babylon had a
vivió   mil   ciudad   Babilonia
hundred gates.
puerta

9. My uncle was a (2) small (1) man of three feet
   tio   era   pequeño
and a half of stature. They had travelled seven miles
   medio estatura   ᴀ habian caminado
and a half. [It is] a year and a half since his father died,
   media   hace   que su   murió
and (2) left (1) him a million and a half a year.
   dexó   le

10. He was a bachelor from Alcala, an excellent
    ᴀ era   bachiller   excelente
master for a [gentleman's son!] What a droll idea!
maestro para un hijo de familia   que gracioso
What a day of affliction for that unhappy mother!
                           para aquella
[Every thing] has prospered in his hands. What a
   todo   ha prosperado   sus mano
blessing from heaven! We never saw so intrepid a
bendicion cielo   intrépido
general, such a destructive artillery, or so complete a
              destructivo artilleria   completo
defeat.
derrota

11. He lived like a man who despised human gran-
           vivió   que despreciaba   gran-
deur, and died like a Christian.
deza   murió   Cristiano

Promiscuous Exercises.

A just king ought to sacrifice himself to the innume-
 justo   debe ᴀ sacrificarse
rable cares which are annexed to government. The
—— cuidado que estan anexo   gobierno

OF ADJECTIVES.

German tongue is more difficult than the English tongue.
Aleman lengua es mas dificultoso que   Ingles
Young men ought always to speak with much discretion.
jóven ▲ deben siempre ▲ hablar ———
Love thy God above all things. The famous ball and
ama á tu   sobre todo cosa   famoso bayle
supper which were given on the occasion. No man
cena   que   se   dió   en ———
can be truly happy till after the last
puede ser verdaderamente feliz hasta despues de postrero
day of his life. Mr. Burke wrote not only on the
día m. *su vida Señor Burke escribió no solo sobre*
sublime, but on the beautiful. His work was entitled
——— *sino   hermoso   su obra se intitulaba*
An Abridgement of Sacred History. Blessed are
   Compéndio   Sagrada Historia bienaventurado son
the merciful, for they [shall obtain] mercy. The
  misericordioso porque   alcanzarán misericordia
Centurion was the captain of a company of a hundred men.
——— *era   capitan   compañia   ciento*
Atrocious crimes deserve severe punishments. French
  atroz   crímen   merecen   severo   castigo
wines [paid duty] [at the rate] of fifty pounds a butt.
    adeudaban   á razon   bota
He was seated on an (2) easy (1) chair. Youth is
▲ *estaba sentado en   poltron   silla juventud es*
presumptuous. Valour, in certain circumstances, is vice's
 presuntuoso   valor   cierto circunstancia es vicio
sword, and virtue's shield.
espada   virtud escudo

COMPARATIVES.

Rule 26. Adjectives are compared with the adverbs *mas*, more; *ménos*, less; and *tan*, so or as: example, *Mas rico*, richer; *ménos vano*, less vain; *tan sábio*, so or as wise.

If the adventure [did not make me] wiser, [at least]
  lance   no me hizo   sábio   á lo menos

it (2) made (1) me more circumspect. We saw innocence
ᴀ   *hizo*   *me*   *circunspecto*   ᴀ *vimos inocencia*
less sheltered and crime more protected. The states
    amparado   *crímen*   *protegido*   *estado*
in which sovereigns are more absolute are those in
  los quales   *son*   *absoluto son aquellos*
which they are less powerful.
          ᴀ *son*   *poderoso*

Note a.—Many are the imaginary troubles of man,
              son   *imaginaria*   *pena*
but the [real ones] are not so many. If men were
pero   *verdadero son no*   *si hombres fueran*
not so ambitious [they would not have] so many
no   .   *no tendrian*
enemies.
enemigo

Rule 27. *Than* after comparatives in English is *que* in Spanish, unless it precedes the pronoun *what*, expressed or understood, and then it is *de:* as—Richer *than* I, *mas rico* que *yo;* More *than* they [or *than* what they] thought, *mas* de *lo que pensaron.*

Wisdom and modesty [do not obtain] less the esteem
    sabiduria   *modéstia no se grangean*   *estimacion*
of men, than pride and folly their contempt. The
                      locura su menosprécio
marquis, said Laura, is a generous man, who [will do]
marques dixo——— *es*   *generoso*   *que hará*
more than he has promised. His fortunate cures were
           ha prometido sus afortunado cura fueron
extolled more than they deserved. [It is better] to be
celebrado   ᴀ   *merecian*   *mas vale* ᴀ *ser*
poor than ignorant, because the sciences are more pre-
pobre   *ignorante porque*   *son*   *pre-*
cious than riches.
cioso

OF ADJECTIVES.

Note a.—Some men are not more than what they
        alguno   *son no*   *lo que* ▲
appear; but others appear more than what they are.
parecen pero otro
Those who have not more than what they want, are
 los que tienen no   *necesitan*
not truly poor.
  verdaderamente pobre

Note b.—The consumption of wheat in London is more
              consumo   *trigo*   *Londres es*
than five millions and ninety thousand bushels a year.
                                      fanega
Saturn is more than twenty-nine years in making its
Saturno echa   .*en hacer su*
revolution; but Mercury is not more than eighty-seven
———— *pero Mercurio echa*
days. We travelled more than half a league.
    ▲ *caminamos*   *legua*

Rule 28. *As* after comparatives is *como:* example,—As beautiful *as* vain, *tan hermosa como vana;* I read as much *as* I write, *tanto leo como escribo.*

It is as easy to do good as to do evil. Nothing
▲   *fácil* ▲ *hacer bien* ▲   *mal nada*
delights so much as the works of nature. Riches are
deleita   *obra*   *naturaleza riqueza son*
not so valuable as virtue, yet men value riches
no apreciable   *sin embargo* *estiman*
more than virtue. Commerce is as useful as war is
              comercio   *útil*
destructive.
destructivo

Note a.—[I was sorry] to leave Fenicia and Dorothea,
     sentí   ▲ *dexar á* ———— ————
whom I loved as much as one woman is capable of
á quienes ▲ *amaba*   *es capaz*

loving another. Liars are as dangerous as contemp-
amar á otra embustero son peligroso despre-
tible. [Do not covet] riches, they are as troublesome as
ciable no codicies ▲ incómodo
dangerous.

Note b.—The more we love an object, the nearer we
▲ amamos objeto próximo ▲
are to hate it. The more they tormented the
estamos á aborrecerle martirizaban á
Christians, the more their number increased. The more
Cristiano su número crecia
we observe a hive of bees, the more wonders
▲ observamos colmena abeja maravilla
we discover.
▲ descubrimos

Note c.—The world is so full of temptations as
mundo está lleno tentacion
[to require] our constant vigilance. So great [will be]
requiere nuestra constante vigilancia será
their joy as (2) [to make] (1) them desire that it never
su gozo hará les desear que ▲ nunca
[may have] an end. So vigorous was the resistance, as
tenga fin vigoroso fué resistencia
[to oblige] the besiegers to abandon the siege.
obligó á sitiador á abandonar sitio

Note d.—War is as destructive, and often more
guerra es destructivo amenudo
destructive, than the plague. Kings are sometimes wiser,
peste f. son sábio
and often as wise, as their ministers.
sus ministro

SUPERLATIVES.

Rule 29. English superlatives ending in *est* or formed by *most* are rendered by prefixing the definite article to the Spanish comparative; as—The wisest, *el mas sábio;* The most ungrateful, *la mas ingrata.*

OF ADJECTIVES.

King Alphonsus put an end to one of the happiest and
   Alfonso dió   *dichoso*
longest reigns that Spain had seen. Self-love is
largo reynado   habia visto
more artful than the most artful of men. Wisdom is
     artificioso
the most precious of all gifts. Cicero was the most
       precioso   *fué*
eloquent of all the Roman orators.
eloqüente   orador

    Note *a*.—We saw accomplished (1) the (3) most
           A   *vimos consumado*
impolitic and most detestable (2) plan that the vilest
impolítico   que   vil
of perfidies could suggest. The opinions of the most
   perfidia pudo sugérir   opinion
enlightened understandings are sometimes errors, and
ilustrado   entendimiento son   error
the most prudent actions pass sometimes for faults.
        prudente accion pasan   por yerro
Self-love is the most formidable enemy of man.

    Note *b*.—Most friends (2) disgust (1) us with friend-
                  amigo   disgusta   nos de amis-
ship, and most devotees with devotion. Rest is agreeable
    tad   devoto   descanso es agradable
to most men. The body of man is [externally] more
               cuerpo   es en el exterior
delicate than that of most animals. Most women em-
delicado   el   animal   muger em-
ploy most of their youth in trifles.
plean   su juventud   friolera

    Note *c*.—He was not the most graceful nor the most
                                    ayroso
agreeable figure in the world. The soul of man is the
agradable figura   es
greatest wonder in the universe.
                  universo

Rule 30. Superlatives which in English are made with *very*, are formed in Spanish by prefixing *muy* to the adjective, or by affixing to it the termination *ísimo;* as—Very clever, *muy hábil,* or *habilísimo;* very easy, *muy fácil,* or *facilísimo.*

A challenge was the result of that very mean
    desafio   fué   resulta   aquella   ruin
action. We traversed those very fruitful fields, and
———   A *atravesamos aquellos   fertil campo*
arrived at last at their very useful manufactory.
llegamos al fin   su   fábrica

Note *a.*—Experience is the best adviser. Solomon
    experiencia es   consejero Salomon
was a very wise king, who manifested very great patience,
fué   sábio   mostró   grande
even seeing himself reduced to very great misery.
         viendose reducido   bajo
Job was a very rich and a very pious prince.
——— *fué   rico   A   virtuoso*
Hercules was very strong. The Alps are very high
——— *fué   fuerte   Alpe son   alto*
mountains.
monte

Note *c.*—He was more king of his kingdom than of his
                    su   reyno
palace. He was a great enemy to pomp, and no less a
palacio   era   pompa
friend to temperance.
    templanza

Government of Adjectives.

Rule 31. Adjectives generally require *de* before their regimen, if it is part of the noun with which they agree; as—*Un cuchillo boto de punta,* a knife blunt at the point; *Un hombre baxo de cuerpo,* a man low in stature.

OF ADJECTIVES.

The dresses of his soldiers (2) made (1) them appear
  vestido sus soldado hacian les parecer
long in the body and short in the legs. Nothing less
largo A *cuerpo corto* A *pierna nada*
than the patience of Job is requisite to teach those
  paciencia —— es necesario para enseñar á los
who are hard of understanding. Blessed are the poor
que son duro entendimiento bienaventurado son pobre
in spirit, for theirs is the kingdom of heaven.
espíritu porque de ellos es reyno los cielos

Rule 32. Adjectives govern their regimen with *en,* if it denotes that wherein the quality of the adjective is conspicuous; as,—*Un hombre constante en sus devociones, y devoto en sus oraciones,* a man constant in his devotions, and devout in his prayers.

Be diligent in thy business and [every thing] [will
sé diligente tus negocios todo
prosper] in thy hands. What is (3) man (1) of
prosperará mano que es
(2) himself, but a soul in [every thing] miserable; in
 sí sino un alma todo ——
his counsels blind; in his works vain; in his appetites
sus consejo ciego obra vano apetito
filthy; in his desires wild; and, finally, in all his
súcio deseo desvariado finalmente todo
things little, and only in his estimation great!
cosa pequeño solamente —— grande

Note *a.*—His civility and his genius inexhaustible in
  su civilidad ingenio inagotable
inventing ways to [please me], contributed to my
inventar médio de complacerme contribuyeron á mi
ruin, and [I thought myself] fortunate in having deposited
pérdida me creía feliz haber depo-
sited my trust in a person of so much integrity.
sitado confianza sujeto integridad

Rule 33. If the regimen of the adjective is the

OF ADJECTIVES.

noun to which the quality of the adjective is directed, it is generally preceded by *á;* as,—*La tiranía es aborrecible á las gentes,* tyranny is hateful to the people.

Nothing is so pleasing to the mind as the light of
      es   agradable   espíritu   luz f.
truth. The sacrifices of Abel were agreeable to the
verdad   sucrificio —— fueron
Lord. His blood [will be] very grateful to the shade
   su sangre f. *será   grato   sombra*
of that hero. [He showed himself] very thankful for
 aquel héroe   se mostró   agradecido
what we had done for him. The dog is faithful to
lo que A *habiamos hecho por él   perro es fiel*
man. She was very fond of wine.
           aficionado vino

Rule 34. If the noun which forms the regimen is also what produces the quality implied in the adjective, it is generally governed with *de;* as,—*Ella estaba pálida de miedo,* she was pale with fear; *Abochornado de la pregunta,* hurt at the question.

Cain, envious of the prosperity of Abel, (2) killed
  —— *envidioso   mató*
(1) him. He remained astonished at her beauty. The
   le A *quedó admirado   su hermosura*
seretary showed himself [something] hurt at these
secretario   algo resentido estas
expressions. [Seldom] are men satisfied with their
expresiones   rara vez están satisfecho   su
condition.

Note a.—She [could not reply], so hurt was
        Ella no pudo replicar abochornado estaba
she at seeing their conduct. Men act not only as if
 A   *ver   su conducta   obran no solamente si*

OF ADJECTIVES.

they were afraid of being virtuous, but ashamed
A *estuvieran temeroso* *virtuoso mas avergonzado*
of [appearing so.]
parecerlo

Rule 35. Numeral adjectives govern with the preposition *de* a noun of dimension; as,—*Treinta pies de alto*, thirty feet high; *seis pulgadas de grueso*, six inches thick.

London-bridge is nine hundred feet in length, forty
    puente tiene   *largo*
in height, and seventy-three in width. To comme-
alto   *ancho para conme-*
morate the fire of London, the inhabitants erected a
morar   *incéndio*   *habitante edificaron*
monument of two hundred feet in height. Noah built
monumento   *pié alto Noé hizo*
an ark of three hundred cubits in length, fifty in breadth,
arca   *codo largo*   *ancho*
and thirty in height.

Note *b*.—The famous mine of Potosi is more than five
       famoso mina —— *es*
hundred feet in depth. The walls of Babylon were
    pies profundo   *muralla Babilonia eran*
two hundred feet high, and fifty broad. What separates
       alto   *ancho que separa á*
the crew of a vessel from death, except a plank
 tripulacion   *navio*   *muerte* f. *sino*   *tabla*
very few inches thick?
poco pulgada grueso

Rule 36. Adjectives denoting *plenty* or *scarcity*, *care* or *negligence*, govern their regimen with *de*; as,—*Un jarro lleno de agua*, a jug full of water; *un hombre falto de juicio*, a man void of reason; *un hombre cuidadoso de su dinero*, a man careful of his money.

His discourses are always clear of superfluous words.
su discurso estar siempre limpio superfluo palabra
An orator ought to avoid all the words which are foreign
debe á evitar que son ageno
to the purpose. They came loaded with booty. The
propósito á venian cargado botin
world is a house full of smoke [in which nothing can be
lleno humo en la que nada se puede
seen]. Solomon was endowed with wisdom, and Abraham
ver fué dotado sabiduria Abrahan
with faith.
fé

Rule 37. Adjectives denoting *desire* or *disdain*, *knowledge* or *ignorance*, *capacity* or *incapacity*, *worthiness* or *unworthiness*, *innocence* or *guilt*, require also *de* before their regimen; as,—*Deseoso de la vida*, desirous of life; *incierto de las conseqüencias*, uncertain of the consequences; *digno de una corona*, worthy of a crown; *reo de muerte*, guilty of death.

[I shall not be responsible] for the consequences. Most
no seré responsable resulta
of our actions are more deserving censure than praise.
son digno vituperio alabanza
Men [would be] less desirous of life [were they] certain
serian deseoso si estuvieran cierto
of a happy death.
feliz muerte f.

Note a.—Their general was incapable of directing the
su —— era incapaz dirigir
movements. The humble Christian scarcely thinks himself
movimiento apénas se crée
worthy to [lift up] his eyes to heaven.
levantar los ojos cielo

Rule 38. *Numeral* and *ordinal* adjectives *super-*

latives, *relatives*, *interrogatives*, and *indefinites*, as well as *nouns used partitively*, require also their regimen with *de;* as,—*El primero de los dos,* the first of the two; *qualquiera de las hijas,* any one of the daughters; *algunos de los oyentes,* some of the hearers.

One of the thieves who had been a surgeon
    ladron que habia sido cirujano
examined the wounds. Three of the most formidable
reconoció herida
enemies with which man is surrounded, are the world,
enemigo de que está rodeado son
the devil, and the flesh. There were two roads, but I
demonio carne f. *habia camino pero*
knew not which of the two [I was to take].
no sabia qual habia de tomar

Rule 39. Adjectives denoting *fitness* or *unfitness* govern their regimen with *para;* as,—*Apto para el empleo,* fit for the employment; *impropio para su edad,* improper for his age.

No one is fit for friendship who is not endowed
ninguno es propio amistad que está no dotado
with virtue. The protection of the arts and sciences is
  virtud
indispensable to the prosperity of a kingdom. A pacific
              pacífico
king is not adapted for great conquests.
 es apropósito conquista

Note a.—These mean artifices are insufficient to
   estos mezquino artificio son insuficiente
impart any progress to the concerted plan. The ox
dar alguno progreso concertado
is not so adequate as the horse to carry burdens. The
es no apto caballo llevar carga

longest reign is short to remedy the errors committed
largo reynado es   remediar   yerro cometido
at the beginning.
á principio

Note b.—True glory is incompatible with inhu-
         verdadero   es   inhu-
manity.
manidad

Rule 40. Adjectives denoting *facility*, or *difficulty*, require *á* before their regimen; as,—*Increible á muchos,* incredible to many; *flexíble á la razon,* yielding to reason.

This secret [remained] impenetrable to all my compa-
este secreto se quedó   mis compa-
nions. They were men inaccessible to pity. [We saw
fiero   A eran   inaccesible   piedad   nos vi-
ourselves] compelled to the greatest humiliations.
mos   obligado   humillacion

Note *a* and *b.*—The meanness of thy birth, said the
                  baxeza   tu nacimiento dixo
Count, is an obstacle very easy to [be overcome]. The
Conde es impedimento fácil   superarse
diseases of children are difficult to cure. See
enfermedad   niño   difícil   curar   ved
here the son of a king reduced to solicit slavery.
aquí al   reducido solicitar servidumbre f.
[He saw himself] compelled to [give up], fearing
   se vió   precisado   rendirse temiendo
some accident.
alguno accidente

Rule 41. Adjectives denoting *profit* or *disprofit, likeness* or *unlikeness,* require *á* before their regimen; as,—*Provechoso á la salud,* advantageous to health; *semejante á su padre,* like his father.

OF ADJECTIVES.

The ambition of princes is often pernicious to their
  — ——   es amenudo pernicioso   sus
subjects. I intend to marry thee to a lady whose
vasallo ▲ *pienso* ▲ *casar* *te con* *dama cuya*
nobility is equal to [mine]. The shadow is the daughter
nobleza es igual la mia   *sombra*
of the sun and of light, but a daughter which is not
                 luz f.   *que es na*
like   her parents.
semejante sus padre

Rule 42. Adjectives denoting *proximity* generally have their regimen with *á*; as,—*Cercano á la muerte*, approaching death; *junto á la casa*, adjoining the house.

He feared that a monarchy so contiguous to that of
▲ *temia que monarquía*   *vecino*   *la*
Asturias [would be] a source of many wars. Some-
        seria manantial   *guerra alguno*
times [we become] slaves, wishing to avoid the evils
vez f. *nos hacemos esclavo queriendo* ▲ *evitar*   *mal*
annexed to war.
anexo

Note a.—He relieved numerous families who were
         ▲ *socorrió á numeroso familia que estaban*
ready to perish. I am ready to give thee the half.
próximo perecer ▲ *estoy pronto dar te mitad*

Rule 43. Adjectives denoting *distance* have generally *de* before their regimen; as,—*Distante de la corte*, distant from court.

The heart of man ought always to be unattached to
                debe siempre ▲ *estar desprendido*
all human grandeur. Neither the king nor the subject
  humano grandeza   *ni*   *ni*   *vasallo*

OF ADJECTIVES. 43

lives independent of the law. In the best state of health
viven independientes   *salud*
[we are not] so far from death as [we think].
  no estamos   *distantes*   *nos imaginamos*

Note a.—The world, far from rewarding virtue,
                          lejos   *premiar*
(2) oppresses (1) it frequently.
   oprime   *la con freqüencia*

Rule 44. Adjectives denoting *behaviour*, govern generally the noun to which it is directed, with *con*; as,—*Ingrato con los amigos*, ungrateful to his friends.

Adrastus, king of the Daunians, was impious towards
 Adrasto   *Daunenses fué impio*
the gods and deceitful towards men. Scipio Africanus
    dios   *pérfido*   *Scipion Africano*
was respectful to his mother, affable to his friends,
fué respetuoso   *su*   *afable*   *amigo*
kind to his domestics, and attentive to all.
bondadoso   *doméstico*   *atento*   *todo*

Promiscuous Exercises.

Impiety is as fatal to a state as to religion. The
impiedad es   *fatal*   *estado*
sciences (2) were (1) not then so much cultivated,
ciencia   *estaban*   *entonces* ▲ *cultivado*
nor riches so little esteemed. Most animals have more
ni riqueza poco apreciado   *animal tienen*
agility than man. The shorter the day is, the longer is
agilidad   *corto*   *es*   *largo*
the night. The most fortunate wars are the greatest
 noche f.   *afortunado guerra son*
scourge of nations. My mother (2) was (1) not milder
azote   *mi madre*   *era*   *no dulce*
than her husband. It seemed that the plague had
   su marido   ▲ *parecia que*   *peste* f. *habia*

entered   Valladolid, so many were the funerals. I
[*entrado en*] ———   *eran   entierro*
chose the city of Valencia, because its climate is one
escogí   ciudad   ——— *porque su temple es*
of the mildest in Spain. A glorious death is preferable
    benigno   glorioso   es preferible
to a shameful life. The evils of war are greater
      vergonzoso   mal   guerra son
than men think. The prince who is faithful to his
       piensan   que es fiel   sus
allies [will be] beloved, not feared by them. He
aliado será   amado no temido de ellos
advanced to [succour them], almost certain of the vic-
avanzó   socorrer los   casi ~ cierto
tory. The ox is   suited   to the culture of the
       buey es proporcionado   cultivo
ground. Fortune is capricious and inconstant in war.
tierra   es caprichoso é inconstante
The errors of princes are difficult to remedy.
   error   son difícil   remediar

PERSONAL PRONOUNS.*
Place of the Pronouns.

Rule 45. The subject or nominative case precedes verbs which are not in the imperative, nor used interrogatively; as,—Tú *hablas*, thou speakest; *vengan* ellos, let *them* come; ¿*viene* ella? is *she* coming?

When he said I am, they [went back] and   fell
quando   dixo   retrocedieron   cayeron
on the ground. All the affections which we rule are
en ᴀ *tierra   afecto   que   regimos son*
lawful. Thou, he, and she will go. They will not
legítimo   ireis   quieren no

* See Grammar. p. 111.

PERSONAL PRONOUNS.

hear his voice.* Why (2) has she accused (1) him
oir su voz   porque   ha ella acusado   le
unjustly? Wilt thou not pardon her at this time?
injustamente quieres   perdonar la esta vez

Note a.—I am the Lord thy God, who [has brought
        soy   tu   que te ha sacado
thee out] of the land of Egypt. The daughter and the
      tierra Egipto   hija
nieces were in the same room; she played and they
sobrina estaban   mismo quarto   tocaba
danced.
baylaban

Note b.—Darina bewailed her misfortunes, her sons
      ——— *lloraba sus desgracia sus hijo*
[manifesting themselves] insensible. Never, perhaps,
  mostrandose   ———   *nunca quizá*
shall I pass (3) so (4) terrible (1) a (2) night! Oh,
   A *pasaré* ———   *o*
human life, exclaimed she, how replete art thou with
      exclamó quan lleno estás
capricious adventures! At sight of the fresh dish, the
caprichoso aventura á vista   nuevo plato
eyes of the parasite sparkled with joy.
ojo   parasito brillaron de alegria

Note c.—It is difficult to define love. Is it possible!
      es difícil A *definir amor es posible*
[said I to myself]. It is easier to avoid an injury
me decia yo á mí mismo es fácil A *evitar injuria*
than [to revenge it] afterwards. It snowed this morning
    vengarla   despues   nevó esta
and now it rains.
ahora llueve

Rule 46. The objective case, when not preceded

* See Observation on Verbs used interrogatively and negatively Grammar, p. 73.

by a preposition, is affixed to infinitives, imperatives, and gerunds; as,—*amar*la, to love *her;* *amemos*la, let us love her; *amando*la, loving *her;* *habiendo*la *amado,* having loved her.

[We must think] of helping thee, Gil Blas. The
hemos menester pensar en ayudar te —— ——
judge hearing her, and having observed her attentively.
juez oyendo la habiendo observado la atentamente
Forgive them, for they know not what they do.
perdona los porque saben no lo que hacen
We can not have any idea of human felicities,
podemos no tener ninguno —— *felicidad*
without having ever experienced them.
sin haber nunca experimentado las

Note a.—[Let us arm ourselves], and [let us endeavour]
armemos nos esforzemos nos
to repel them with intrepidity. Conduct yourselves
á rechazar los con intrepidez portad os
with respect.
respeto

Rule 47. Verbs which are not in the infinitive, imperative, nor gerund, have generally the objective case prefixed; as,—*El* me *enseña,* he teaches *me; yo* lo *digo,* I say *it; nosotros* los *oimos,* we hear *them.*

God sees us, calls to us, and [will judge] us. All
ve nos llama á juzgará
the affections which rule us are criminal. He that
afecto que rigen son culpable el que
[wishes for] the sceptre does not know it, and how shall
desea cetro á no conoce le como
he discharge his duties, not knowing them?
desempeñará sus obligacion conociendo las

Note a.—These words comforted me much. I
estas palabras consolaron me mucho

PERSONAL PRONOUNS.

diverted them with the account of my last adventure. I
diverti   los   relacion   mi último aventura
took her to her country, where [we were married].
llevé la   su tierra donde   nos casamos

Note b.—We come to see her. He will endeavour
            venimos á ver la   procurará
to deceive us. Death only [shall be able] to
▲ engañar nos   solamente   podrá   ▲
separate us.
separar

Variety in the Use of the Objective Cases.

Rule 48. Prepositions when expressed always govern the second objective case; as,—*Sin tí,* without *thee;* contra ellos, against *them.*

It is better to leave the great than to complain of
es   ▲ dexar á   ▲ quexarse
them. If God is for us, we are enough to go against
        si   es   somos bastantes para ir contra
them. I [shall go] with him. Will you come with us?
      iré   quiere vm. venir
He could not live without her.
    podia   vivir

Note a.—Speak little with others, and much with
          habla poco con otros   mucho
[thyself]. He speaks to himself when he is alone.
tí   habla con sí quando está solo

Note c.—I love him more than her. We esteem
      quiero le   que á   apreciamos
her less than him. Companions, the king has received
la menos   compañeros   ha recibido
you with more attention than me; but he has rewarded
os   atencion   pero   premiado
me more than you.
me

PERSONAL PRONOUNS.

Rule 49. When in English the objective case of the first or second person is the regimen of the verb, or of the preposition *to* expressed or understood, we use the first case; as,—I exhorted *thee, yo* te *exhorté;* he conquered *me, el* me *venció.*

God [will judge] us. Let her reward me. What
Dios juzgará recompensa lo que
I had heard seemed to me a dream. They brought
habia oido parecia sueño traxeron
me a piece of black bread. Ye are spies, and we
pedazo negro pan sois espia
[will punish] you.
castigarémos

Rule 50. If the objective case of the third person is the regimen of the English verb, we translate it by *le, los* for the masculine, *la, las* for the feminine, and *lo* for the neuter; as, He killed *him, el* le *mató;* she saw *them, ella* los *vió;* they heard *it, ellos* lo *oyéron.*

Moses touched with his rod the water of the river,
Moises tocó su vara rio
and changed it into blood. [Hearken unto] the words
convirtió en sangre escucha palabra
which [I am going] to tell thee, and engrave them
que voy á decir graba
deeply in thy memory. Man ought to shun
profundamente en tu memoria debe A *evitar*
[every thing that] can divert him from the love of
todo lo que puede divertir amor
God.

Rule 51. If the third person in English be governed by the preposition *to* expressed or understood, we render it by *le, les* for both genders; as, We spoke *to him, nosotros* le *hablamos;* I wrote *to her, yo* le *escribí;* she told *them, ella* les *dixo.*

PERSONAL PRONOUNS. 49

Canst thou pass a day without thinking on thy Cre-
  puedes pasar   sin pensar en tu Cri-
ator, without giving him thanks, without worshipping
ador   dar gracia   adorar
him? Generosity unites many virtues, and gives them
  generosidad junta   da
an heroical energy.
 heróico energia

Notes *a* and *b*.—The best of kings do the harm which
      mejor hacen mal que
they would not, because flatterers disguise it to
  querrian porque lisonjero disfrazan *
them. Husbands, says Saint Paul, love your wives,
    marido dice santo Pablo amad á vuestras muger
God has given them to you. Her image presented itself
 ha dado   su imágen presentaba se
[to them] without ceasing. I shall demand my liberty,
 les sin cesar pediré mi libertad
and they will grant it me. God demands thy heart;
  concederán   Dios requiere tu
canst thou refuse it to him? The king granted them
puedes rehusar   concedió
the privileges, but he did not grant them to them for a
 *privilegio *á* concedió   por*
long time.
mucho tiempo

Notes *c* and *d*.—The death which Lucretia gave her-
       que ——— *dió*
self, made her immortal. The employment was not
 hizo inmortal   exercicio fué no
less profitable to him than to me. But as she loved
          pero como amaba
him as much as he loved her, they were happy.
        eran feliz

Note *e*.—The Athenians understand what is right,
  Ateniense conocen lo que es justo

---
* See note *e*.

but the Lacedemonians practise it. I solicited her hand,
mas   Lacedemonio practican   solicité   su
she denied it; I offered her my fortune, she refused it;
negó   ofrecí   caudal   rehusó
I entreated her to write, she granted it.
rogué   que escribiese   concedió

Promiscuous Exercises.

Give her this letter, and give it her before
da   esta carta   des   delante de
him. Few people prefer the censure which is useful
poco gente f. *prefieren   censura que es util*
to them, to the praises which betray them. We
alabanza que venden
ought to relieve the poor when we can do it.
debemos á *socorrer á   quando podemos hacer*
We always love [those who] admire us. In
siempre amamos á aquellos que admiran   en
thee have I put my trust. I invited him to sup
he á *puesto mi confianza   convidé   á cenar*
with me. Truth is agreeable, [let us seek] it.
con   verdad es agradable   busquemos
Remember (2) that (1) ye are mortal. Prosperity
acordad   que   os sois   prosperidad
gets us friends, and adversity tries them.
grangea   amigo   adversidad prueba

POSSESSIVE PRONOUNS.*

Rule 52. Possessives always agree in gender, number, and case, with the possession; as,—*Nuestro jardin*, our garden; *en vuestras quintas*, in your villas.

Rule 53. Possessive pronouns when used as pronominal adjectives precede the noun with which they agree; as,—*Nuestros empeños*, our endeavours; *vuestras virtudes*, your virtues.

* See Grammar, p. 116.

POSSESSIVE PRONOUNS.

Our virtues are frequently no more than disguised
son freqüentemente no disfrazado
vices. I exhort you, gentlemen, to continue your lite-
vicio exhorto os á continuar lite-
rary labours. Can ye abandon your wives, your
rario trabajo podeis abandonar muger
children, your king, your country? It seems that the
hijo patria parece que
first men [lost sight of] the laws of nature:
primero perdieron de vista
hence sprang our errors, our crimes, our enemies,
de aquí nacieron error crímen enemigo
our wars. [No one] thinks to scrutinize our origin
guerra nadie piensa en escudriñar orígen
nor the occurrences of our life [as long as] we do not
ni circunstancia en tanto que á
endeavour to become superior to our companions.
nos empeñamos en hacernos ——— compañero

Rule 54. *Mio, tuyo,* and *suyo,* lose their last syllable when placed before the noun; as,—*Mi conducta,* my conduct; *tus hazañas,* thy exploits.

The sun and the moon [will lose] their light, and the
perderán
dead [will arise] and [come out] of their sepulchres.
muerto resuscitarán saldrán sepulcro
Old Alberto, their father, pressed them in his arms,
anciano ——— estrechaba brazo
promising to crown very soon their tenderness. Jupiter
ofreciendo á coronar pronto ternura ———
performs its revolution [round] the sun attended
da vuelta al rededor de acompañado
by its satellites. They parted my garments among
de satélite repartiéron vestido entre
themselves, and upon my vesture they cast lots.
sí sobre vestidura echaron suerte

Rule 55. *Mio* is placed after in our addresses, that is, when it agrees with the second person; as,—

D 2

¡ *Acuérdate, hijo mio!* remember, my son! ¡ *venzamos, paisanos mios!* let us conquer, my countrymen!

[Let us lay aside] flattery, my friends. [Say no
dexémonos de   adulacion   amigo   no digas
more,] my dear, replied my brother to his wife.
mas   querido replicó   hermano
[Figure to thyself,] my James, the pleasure with which
figúrate   Diego   gusto   que
I heard these words. Thou beginnest now, my son, to
oí estas   comienzas ahora   á
enjoy an agreeable life. My good sir, you are en-
gozar.   á señor vm. está en-
tirely mistaken.
teramente equivocado

Rule 56. When possessives are used as pronouns they agree in gender, number, and case, with the noun which they represent, and are preceded by the definite article; as,—*Tu casa y* la mia, thy house and mine; *de mis esfuerzos y* los tuyos, of my efforts and *thine.*

When the Romans knew the utility of the Spanish
quando   Romano conocieron   utilidad   Español
sword, they abandoned theirs. I have paid my expenses,
espada   abandonaron   he pagado   gasto
[let them pay] theirs. The historian relates that their
que paguen   historiador refiere que
  manners   differ from ours. They have their
costumbre f. *diferencian   tienen*
opinion, and we ours. [As soon as] that robber had
dictámen   luego que aquel ladron hubo
finished his history, another began his, saying, the
acabado   otro comenzó   diciendo
histories which [we have just heard] are not so curious
       que   acabamos de oir   son no   curioso
as mine.

POSSESSIVE PRONOUNS.

Rule 57. When the possessive pronoun is connected with the noun by a verb, the article is omitted; as,—*Este libro es* mio, this book is *mine:* el palacio es suyo, the palace is *his*.

The house is ours, but the garden is theirs. They say
         es   *pero*   *es*   *dicen*
that his army was beaten; but I say that victory never
      exército fué vencido   *digo*   *victoria nunca*
was theirs, it always was ours. The colonies which now
      siempre   *colónia que ahora*
are theirs, were [formerly] ours, and the ships which
son   *fueron en otro tiempo*   *navio que*
are ours have been theirs.
     han sido

Rule 58. When *mine, thine,* &c. are preceded by *of,* we omit the preposition and article, and place the possessive after the noun; as,—*Un amigo* mío, a friend *of mine;* un autor nuestro, an author *of ours*.

O thou, said she to him, whose tears softened the
  ó   *decia*   *cuyas lágrimas ablandaron*
hardness of this honest heart of mine! Be not a slave
dureza *este honesto*   *seas no esclavo*
of hers. My coming has been to visit two aunts of
         venida ha sido para visitar á   *tia*
mine who are ill. An author of ours hath imitated
   que estan enfermo   *ha imitado*
the best poet of theirs.

Observation.—Pilate took water, and washed his hands.
        Pilato tomó   *se lavó*
[I will pierce] my heart with this dagger. David killed
me atravesaré   *esta daga* —— *mató á*
Goliah, and [cut off] his head. Scarcely [had I put]
     cortó   *cabeza* *apénas* *eché*
my foot on the ground, when the innkeeper [came out]
 pié á A *tierra quando* *mesonero* *salió*
to receive me. The said gentleman wore at his side a
á recibir   *tal caballero traia á*   *lado*

long sword. As soon as I extricated my head a
largo chafarote luego que desembaracé cabeza
little, I said to him. Each put a pistol to my breast.
poco dixe cada uno puso pistola pecho
Gracchus divided the treasures of Attalus, but it cost
 Graco repartió tesoro Atalo pero costó
him his life. Saying this, she [took off] from her
 vida diciendo esto sacó de
finger the ring, and put it in my hand. The Philistines
 dedo sortija puso mano Filisteo
took Sampson, and [put out] his eyes. Thy head
prendieron á sacaron
aches, her side aches, and my heart aches. Your
duele costado
highness knows well that the result of these factions
 alteza sabe bien que resultado estas faccion
will be fatal to your interests. Sir, my son is
será funesto para interes señor hijo está
[in love] with your daughter. His servants and yours
enamorado de hija criado
are in prison. Gentlemen, your prodigality and mine
estan la cárcel prodigalidad
have ruined his family.
han arruinado familia

Promiscuous Exercises.

Self-love keeps our eyes always blindfolded. A
amor propio tiene ojo siempre vendado
nephew of hers married a niece of his. Honour thy
sobrino casó con sobrina honra
father and thy mother, that thy days [may be] long
 que dia sean largo
upon the land, which the Lord thy God has given thee.
sobre que ha dado
And Isaac said to his father, My father; and he answered,
 ——— *dixo respondió*
what [do you wish,] my son. When [he had nothing to give]
que quieres quando no tenia nada que dar

RELATIVE PRONOUNS.

he promised, but his were not court promises. He
prometia pero   eran no corte promesa
would not even accept the ring which   truly   was
quiso no aun admitir sortija que verdaderamente era
mine.

RELATIVE PRONOUNS.*

Rule 59. *Quien* relates to persons only, and is always preceded by the preposition *á* when governed by the verb; as, *El rey es* quien *lo manda,* the king (it) is *who* commands it.; *El hombre á* quien *envió, y* con quien *fuimos,* the man *whom he sent,* and *with whom* we went.

Who (2) hath (1) no shame hath no conscience.
           tiene   no vergüenza   conciencia
2 It is (1) He who made man, and who [will reward]
   á es   hizo á   recompensará
him, and we are the sinners whom he calls, and for
          somos   pecador   llama   por
whom he suffered.
       padeció

Rule 60. *Qual* and *que* refer to persons and to things; as,—*El criado* que *vino, y* por el qual *mandé la carta,* the servant *who* came, and *by whom* I sent the letter.

Self-love is the first that exists, and the last that dies
                            existe   último   muere
in the heart of man. The man that fears God, and that
                                  teme á
fears but him, is   truly   free. We do not
     solo á   es verdaderamente libre
reflect   enough on the dangers to which we are
reflexîonamos   estamos
exposed. Death is an evil for which [there is no] remedy.
expuesto   mal para   no hay   remedio

* See Grammar, p. 120.

RELATIVE PRONOUNS.

Rule 61. *Cuyo* also relates both to persons and things, but agrees with the word by which it is immediately followed; as,—*La nacion* cuyo rey *es sábio*, the nation *whose king* is wise; *la calle* cuyas casas *son altas,* the street the *houses of which* are lofty.

The God of armies, whose cause we defend, [will
            exército   *causa*   *defendemos* pro-
protect] us. I placed on the table two kinds of soup, at
tegerá   *puse en* *mesa* *género* *sopa á*
the sight of which they took their places. She feared
   vista   *tomaron* *asiento*   *temia á*
a man whose counsels she could not follow. The
           consejo   *podia* *seguir*
Phœnicians, whose commerce and navigation we had
 Fenicio   *comercio*   *navegacion habiamos*
[so much] admired. Minos, whose wisdom and laws
    tanto admirado *Minos*
had been so revered.
habian sido *reverenciado*

Rule 62. *Who,* having its antecedent expressed in English, is generally rendered by *que,* especially if placed close to the antecedent, and agreeing with it in case; as,—A king *who* governs well, *un rey* que *gobierna bien;* the God *who* created us, *el Dios* que *nos creó.*

We have expelled from the city men who were
   hemos expelido   *ciudad*   *éran*
useless. The most unfortunate of men is a king who
inútil   *desdichado*
believes that his happiness consists in making others
 crée que   *felicidad consiste* *hacer á otros*
miserable. Apollo killed the Cyclops who had forged
       ——— *Apolo*   *Cíclope* *habian forjado*
the thunderbolts of Jupiter.
  rayo

Rule 63. *Whom* is generally translated *quien;*

RELATIVE PRONOUNS.

as,—The man *whom* we saw, *el hombre á* quien *vimos;* the women *whom* I sent, *las mugeres á* quienes *envié*

[I met] with Doctor Sangrado, whom I had not
me encontré ——— Sangredo no
seen since the death of my master. It is difficult to
visto desde amo es difícil A
love those whom we do not esteem. I am one
amar á aquellos A *no estimamos soy*
of those lads whom thou [didst threaten] with the
aquello mozo amenazaste
rack at Cacabelos.
tormento en

Rule 64. If the English antecedent is a personal pronoun, agreeing in case with the relative, it is generally suppressed, and the definite article prefixed to the relative; as,—She *who* wrote, la que *escribió;* we *who* are friends, los que *somos amigos;* they *who* endeavour, los que *se empeñan.* See Demonstratives, Rule 75.

The best Christian is he who knows and practises best
 Cristiano es sabe practica
the law of God. They who forgive much manifest
ley perdonan mucho manifiestan
as much valour as they who resist. They who till the
valor resisten labran
field, says Oliva, are not the slaves of us who dwell
campo dice —— son no esclavo moramos
in the cities, but our parents, since they support us.
sino pues mantienen
I want a [maid-servant], and thou art she who suits
necesito criada eres conviene
me. [Be instructed], ye that judge the earth. Blessed
instruios juzgais bienaventurado
are they who trust in God.
confian en

Rule 65. *Yo* and *tú* must always be expressed

before the relative; as,—Yo que *te amaba, I who* loved thee; tú que *me aborreces, thou who* dost hate me.

O thou who hast left an immense space betwixt
O tú has dexado inmenso espacio entre
thee, and all the presumptuous who aspire to [imitate
                    presuntuoso aspiran á imitarte
thee]. I who [would have given] her [for nothing].
              daria de balde
Thou who seemest [to have been born] to be our
     pareces haber nacido para ser
scourge [listen to] me.
azote escucha

Rule 66. *That* or *which*, is translated *que;* as,—The estate *that* we bought, *la hacienda* que *compramos*.

Let us endeavour to fulfil the duties of the
    procuremos á *cumplir con obligacion*
state in which God has placed us. Lying is a vice
estado ha colocado mentira es vicio
which we cannot sufficiently hate.
no podemos bastante aborrecer

Rule 67. *What* is translated *lo que:* as,—*What* we desire, lo que *deseamos*.

Religion teaches us not only what we ought to
   ———— *enseña solo debemos* á
believe; but what we ought to practise. The king who, to
creer mas á *practicar por*
enlarge his dominions, sheds the blood of his subjects,
extender dominio derrama sangre f. *vasallo*
deserves to lose what he possesses, since he wishes to
merece á *perder posée pues quiere* á
usurp what [does not belong] to him.
usurpar no pertenece

Rule 68. The relative *que* is, generally, placed close to its antecedent, unless the words which intervene form a parenthesis to the sentence; as,—*La dicha espada*

RELATIVE PRONOUNS. 59

cortava como una navaja, y no habia armadura (*por
fuerte y encantada que fuese*) que *se le parase delante,* the said sword cut like a razor, and there
never was an *armour* (so hardened or so powerfully
enchanted) *that* could withstand its edge. — Don
Quixote, b. iii. ch. 18.

That man hath riches sufficient, who hath enough
    el   *tiene riqueza suficiente*   *bastante*
to be charitable. Those men are unworthy to live, who
para ser caritativo   *son indigno vivir*
live only for themselves. Men ought to shun the
viven solo para   *deben* á *evitar*
amusements (however agreeable they may be) which
diversion   *por mas agradable que sean*
corrupt the morals. He is wise, who regulates his
corrompen costumbre f.   *sabio arreglar*
conduct with prudence and justice.

Rule 69. Relatives must immediately follow the
preposition by which they are governed; as, —*El
hombre* con quien *hablamos,* the man *whom* we spoke
with.

Moses was the instrument which God [made use] of
  Moises fué instrumento que se sirvió
to deliver the Israelites. This is what I never thought
para librar Israelitas esto es nunca pensé
of. That was what he stood to. War is the greatest
en eso fué se atuvo á
evil which God afflicts men with.
    que aflige con

Rule 70. Relatives must be expressed, although
only understood in English;—*La muger* que *amo,*
the woman I love; *la pluma* con que *escribo,* the pen
I write with.

The temptations we daily fall into ought to
  tentacion diariamente caemos en deben á

convince us of the dangers the world we live in is
convencer   peligro   vivimos en está
surrounded with. The reward he merits for having
  rodeado   de   prémio   merece por haber
conquered them, is equal to the punishments they deserve
vencido   es igual   castigo   merecen
for [having allowed themselves to be conquered.]
        haberse dexado vencer

INTERROGATIVE PRONOUNS.*

Rule 71. Interrogatives do not admit the article; as,
—¿Quien *viene?* who comes? ¿qual *tengo?* which
have I? ¿que *tenemos?* what have we? ¿cuyos *son
los libros?* whose are the books

Who was the first man? Whom have we offended?
        fué   *hemos   ofendido*
Who were the evangelists? What punishment does he
      fueron   evangelistas   *castigo*   a
deserve? Which of the commandments have we not
merece   *mandamientos hemos*
sinned against? What [shall we do?] Whose riches
pecado contra   *harémos*
will these be? Who [shall comfort] us in that day of
a   *serán*   *consolará*   *aquel*
tribulation?

Note *a.*—Whose is the victory? In whose likeness was
             es   *semejanza fué*
man created? If Adam and Eve were the parents of
  criado   *Adan   Eva fueron*   *padre*
mankind, whose sons are we?
género humano   *hijo somos*

Rule 72. If the interrogation is governed by a
preposition, it must also precede the answer; as,—
¿Con quien *se casa ella?* whom doth she marry?
con *el marques,* the marquis. ¿De que *murio?* what
did he die *of?* de *calentura,* a fever.

* See Grammar, p. 124.

Whom have we offended? God. For whom was
á quien hemos ofendido   para   fué
the world created? For man. What will the queen
              creado   á
travel in? Her coach. What was the law written on?
viajará en   coche   fué   escrito en
Two tables of stone. Whom did the Israelites murmur
     tabla piedra   á   murmuraron
against? Moses.
de

Note a.—Whose sons are we? God's. Whose son was
                      somos   fué
Solomon? David's. Whose father is God? Ours.
                                        es

DEMONSTRATIVE PRONOUNS.*

Rule 73. *This* is translated by the first; as,—I shall gain *this* lawsuit, *ganaré* este *pleyto;* I shall send *these* goods, *mandaré* estos *géneros*.

These were his last words. Are these thoughts,
fueron   último palabra   son   pensamiento
O Telemachus! worthy of the son of Ulysses? He
  Telemaco   digno
delayed the execution until the last stage, this was at
dilató   hasta   posada   fué en
Cacabellos. My father wishes to marry me to this man,
                      quiere á casar   con
but this will never take place.
  á nunca tendrá efecto

Rule 74. *That* may be rendered by the second or third; as,—That letter, *esa* or *aquella carta;* those papers, *esos* or *aquellos papeles.*†

Those evils of which [thou complainest] are caused
        mal   te   quexas   son causado
by those pleasures to which [thou didst give thyself up]
por   placer   te entregaste

* See Grammar, p. 124.
† See also Observation, Grammar, p. 126.

in thy youth. That poverty which thou endurest, and
    juventud   *pobreza*   *padeces*
those misfortunes which he experienced, proceeded from
  desgracia   *experimentó procedieron*
the same cause. That is to what I never shall consent.
 mismo causa   *es en*   *consentiré*

Rule 75. English personal pronouns, followed by a relative, not agreeing in case, are generally resolved by the demonstrative in Spanish; as,—*We* ought to reward him *who* labours for the country, *debemos premiar á* aquel que *trabaja por la patria*.

[Should we not call] an enemy to the republic him
  no llamaríamos   A *enemigo*   *república á*
who [should violate] the laws? thou didst transgress
        violase   *tú* A *quebrantaste*
them; him who [should despise] the authority of the
            menospreciase   *autoridad*
senate? thou didst crush it; him who [should foment]
senado *tú* A *oprimiste*   *fomentase*
seditions? thou didst excite them.
sedicion *tu* A *excitaste*

Rule 76. *That*, used twice in the sentence, is generally translated by *aquel* the second time, if the objects differ in their distance, and by *ese* if they do not; as,—*That* man who is there, and *that* that is yonder, ese *hombre que está ahí, y* aquel *que está allí; that* man, and *that* woman who goes with him, ese *hombre, y* esa *muger que va con él*.

This crown and this sceptre, which we present to
   corona   *cetro*   *presentamos*
your majesty. That smiling aspect, and that affability
           risueño semblante   *afabilidad*
with which your majesty [listens to] the complaints of
                  escucha   *quexa*
your subjects. That body which thou seest covered
 vasallo   *cuerpo*   *ves cubierto*

DEMONSTRATIVE PRONOUNS. 63

with wounds, and that arm which he left on the field of
de herida   brazo   dexó en   campo
battle, proclaim his patriotism.
batalla declaran patriotismo

   Note a.—Saying this, I took off the candle from the
                diciendo   quité   vela
candlestick, and delivering the former to the [old woman]
candelero   entregando   vieja
I handed the latter to Fabricius. As was his life, so was
alargué   como fué   así
his death; he edified as much in the latter, as he had
             edificó   habia
edified in the former.
edificado

   Note b.—The object of elegance is to please; that of
                   objeto   elegancia es ▲ agradar
eloquence is to persuade. This palace, and that which I
eloqüencia ▲ persuadir   palacio
showed you, are the king's.
enseñé   son

   Note c.—The first thing which I did was to leave
                primero cosa   hice fué ▲ dexar
the mule at discretion, that is [to go] at the pace
   mula á ———————   que fuese á   paso
she liked.
   quisiese

Promiscuous Exercises.

The ministers he appointed were clever. Who
    ministro   señaló   eran hábil
soweth contentions reapeth wars. All flatterers live at
siembra discordia coge   lisonjero viven á
the expense of him who [listens to] them. Things do
▲   costa   escucha   ▲
not pass for what they are, but for what they appear
    pasan por   son   parecen
This is the man whom I was with. The exploits
este es   estaba   hazaña

which a predecessor has done are confusion and infamy
——————— ha hecho son ——————— é infámia
to the successor, who does not imitate them. The dog
para sucesor A imita perro
is the only animal whose natural talents are evident,
es único ——————— ——————— talento son patente
and from whose education we always derive much
——————— sacamos
advantage. The body perishes, the soul is immortal;
ventaja cuerpo perece alma es inmortal
nevertheless we [attend to] the former, and [neg-
sin embargo cuidamos de nos des-
lect] the latter. These news which I tell thee,
cuidamos de noticia digo
those reports which [were afloat] [last week], and
voz f. corrieron la semana pasada
those rumours which reached us last year, agree
rumor alcanzaron se acuerdan
wonderfully. What is man in the presence of God?
maravillosamente es en presencia
and whose protection is equal to his? They who sin
——————— es igual pecan
are the slaves of sin.
esclavo

INDEFINITES.

Rule 77. *One* is rendered by *uno*; as,—*One* does not know what to think, *no sabe* uno *que pensar*.

Rule 78. *Somebody, some one, anybody, any one* are rendered by *alguien* or by *alguno* in the singular. as,—Has *anybody* said it? ¿*lo ha dicho* alguien? *some one* may have said it, alguno *puede haberlo dicho*.

Rule 79. *Nobody, no one, not anybody,* or *not any one,* is construed *nadie,* or *ninguno* in the singular; as,—He fears *nobody, á* nadie *teme;* I see *no one, á* ninguno *veo.*

Rule 80. *Something* or *anything*, is *algo*; as,—Hast thou *anything* to say to me? *¿tienes* algo que *decirme?*

Rule 81. *Nothing*, or *not anything*, is translated *nada*; as,—*Not anything* he said convinced her, nada de lo que dixo la convenció.

Rule 82. *Some*, or *any*, is rendered by *alguno* in both numbers, or by *unos*; as,—I want books, have you *any?* me faltan libros, *¿tiene vm*. algunos? do you know *any* of these ladies? *¿conoce vm. á* algunas *de éstas señoras?* I know *some, conozco á* unas.

Rule 83. *None*, or *not any*, is translated *ninguno*; example:—*None* of these ladies is the married daughter, ninguna de estas señoras es la hija casada.

Rule 84. *Whoever, whosoever, whichever,* or *whichsoever*, is translated *quienquiera que,* or *qualquiera que,* in both numbers; as,—*Whoever* thou mayest be, quienquiera *que seas; whoever* may come, qualquiera *que venga.*

Rule 85. *Whatever,* or *whatsoever,* must be expressed by *qualquier cosa que,* as,—*Whatever* I say, qualquier cosa *que digo.*

Rule 86. *Another, other,* or *others*, is rendered by *otro* in both numbers; as,—Send me another, *mándame* otro: these books are dear, but I have others cheaper, *estos libros son caros, pero tengo* otros *mas baratos.*

Rule 87. *Each other* is translated *uno otro;* and *one another, unos otros;* with or without the article, and with the corresponding preposition placed between them; as,—of each other, *el uno del otro,* or *uno de otro.*

Rule 88. *Both* is *ambos,* and *several* is *varios;* as, —Neither of them has written, because *both* are ill,

INDEFINITES.

ní el uno ní el otro ha escrito, por que ambos *estan malos.*

Rule 89. *Much* is construed *mucho*, and *many, muchos;* as,—You think I have no troubles, but I have many, *piensa vm. que no tengo pesadumbres, pero tengo* muchas.

Rule 90. *Each*, when alone, is *cada qual*, or *cada uno;* as,—I have bought six books, *each* in a different language, *he comprado seis libros*, cada uno *en un idioma diferente.*

Rule 91. *Each*, or *every*, if, when joined to a noun, they are synonymous, is expressed by *cada;* as, —He accompanied *every* interrogatory with a very low bow, cada *pregunta la acompañaba con una profunda reverencia.*

Rule 92. *Every*, when not denoting the same meaning as *each*, is translated by *todo* in both its genders and numbers; as,—*Every one* lighted his candle, *encendiéron* todos *sus velas:* he gave them every thing he had, *les dió* todo *lo que tenia.*

Rule 93. *All* is translated *todo* in both its genders and numbers; as,—*All* that glitters is not gold, todo *lo que brilla no es oro;* I invited many, but they did not *all* come, *convidé á muchos, pero no vinieron* todos.

Exercise on the foregoing rules.—One ought not to be
                                            debe   á *ser*
judge and plaintiff in the same cause. The man whom
          demandador   *mismo*
nobody pleases is more unfortunate than the man who
        agrada es   *desdichado*
pleases *nobody.* If *anybody* [should ask] me where he
                      preguntare   *donde*
is, what can I answer him? *No one* is free from
está   *puedo responder*   *está libre*

INDEFINITES. 67

death. [There is] *nothing* wicked or shameful but sin.
　　　　no hay　　　*　　malo ni vergonzoso sino*
Fickle minds begin many things and finish *none*.
variable génio empiezan　　　　　　　no acaban
The innkeeper was as ready to relate all his affairs, as
　　mesonero era　fácil en contar　　　cosa
curious in [informing himself] of those of *others. One*
curioso en　informarse　　　　　　　†
sows the seed, *another* gathers the fruit. Men [ought
siembra semilla　　coge　fruto　　deben
to love] *one another. Many* [deceive] themselves,
amarse á　　　　　　　se engañan á mismo
wishing to deceive *others*. The world is a stage, in
queriendo ▲ *engañar á　　　　　　es　teatro* ✦
which *every one* plays his part. All men, said Captain
　　　　representa papel　　　　　　dixo
Rolando, wish to [appropriate to themselves] the wealth of
　　　　desean ▲　*apropiarse　　　　　bien*
another. Consider, man, that after thy death all thy
　　　considera　　　que despues de
hopes [will have vanished], not even *one* [will remain]
esperanza habrán desvanecido ni aun　　　quedará
to thee. Among authors [there are] *some* who copy
　　　　　　entre　　　　hay　　　copian
literally from *one another,* and *others* who make theirs
literalmente　　　　　　　　　　　　hacen
the thoughts of *others*. Solomon was the most
pensamientos　　　　　Salomon fué
fortunate, and Job the most unfortunate of men:
feliz　　　—　　　　infeliz
　　yet *both* declare that *all* is vanity. Nature
sin embargo ‡ *declaran　　　es vanidad naturaleza*
and religion *both* come from God. *All* God has
　　　　　　‡　*vienen　　　　　　　h‥*
created proclaims his omnipotence. How terrible will
creado proclama　　omnipotencia quan ——— ▲

　　　　＊ See note *a*, to Rule 81, Grammar.
　　　　† See note *a*, to Rule 86, Grammar.
　　　　‡ See note *a*, to Rule 88, Grammar.

INDEFINITES.

(2) death (1) be to *any one* who [has neglected]
              será   *   que se haya descuidado de*
his salvation! To receive from *no one* is inhumanity:
————   *no recibir*   *es inhumanidad*
from *many* meanness; and from *all*, greediness. The
       vileza   *avaricia*
belligerent powers are many, and if *any one* of them
beligerante potencia son   †
should propose any conditions *all* [will be] lost.
A *propusiere*   ————   *será perdido*
[No doubt] the enemy [will ask for] *something* as
no hay duda que   *pedirá*   *como*
an equivalent, but *nothing* [shall we grant] to him,
, equivalente pero   *concederémos*
because *whatever* [we might yield] to him [would not
porque   *cediéramos*   *no con-*
satisfy] his ambition. *Whosoever* [shall persevere]
tentaria   ————   *perseverare*
until the end shall be saved. *Whatever* measures the
hasta fin será salvado   ‡   *medida*
murderer [may take] to flee from himself, his crime
asesino tome para huir   *delito*
will always accompany him. The dead [will arise]
A *siempre acompañará*   *muerto resucitarán*
and *every one* [will appear] before the Judge, who
              parecerán ante
[will reward] *each* [according to] his works. Many wish
premiará á   *segun*   *obra*   *quieren*
to be devout, but *none* wishes to be humble.
     devoto   *quiere*

        * See note *a*, to Rule 78, Grammar.
        † See note *b*, to Rule 78, Grammar.
        ‡ See note *a*, to Rule 84, Grammar.

NAMES OF THE TENSES

To which the Roman Capitals of the following Exercises refer.

Indicative
- A Present.
- B Imperfect.
- C Perfect indefinite.
- D Perfect definite.
- E Pluperfect.
- F Future imperfect.
- G Future perfect.

Imperative
- H Present.

Subjunctive
- I Present.
- K Imperfect
  - 1. in RA
  - 2. in SE
  - 3. in RIA.
- L Perfect.
- M Pluperfect
  - 1. in RA
  - 2. in SE
  - 3. in RIA.
- N Future imperfect.
- O Future perfect.

Infinitive
- P Present.
- Q Perfect.
- R Gerund.
- S Compound of the Gerund.
- T Participle.

On SER and ESTAR.

Rule 94. General truths and the qualities of the mind are expressed with *ser*, and emotions with *estar*; as,—*La muerte es terrible,* death is terrible; *soy humilde,* I am humble; *estás triste,* thou art sorrowful.

Rule 95. The natural beauties of the body, and its defects when deemed permanent, are denoted by *ser*; as,—*La muchacha es bonita,* the girl *is* pretty; *el hijo era feo,* the son *was* ugly; *la madre es coxa,* the mother *is* lame; *el padre es ciego*, the father *is* blind.

Rule 96. The physical changes in the animal body are expressed with *estar;* as,—*El niño está frio*, the child *is* cold (*to the touch*); *estuve coxo la semana pasada*, I *was* lame last week.

Rule 97. The natural qualities of substances, when taken in a general sense, are expressed by *ser;* as,—*El yelo es frio*, ice *is* cold; *la nieve es blanca*, snow *is* white; *la cera es blanda*, wax *is* soft.

Rule 98. The chemical and mechanical changes in substances are expressed with *estar;* as,—*El plomo está derretido*, the lead *is* melted; *la cera estaba dura*, the wax *was* hard.

Rule 99. When *to be* connects two nouns, two pronouns, two infinitives, or one of each, it is translated *ser;* as,—*El temor de Dios es el princípio de la sabiduria*, the fear of God *is* the beginning of wisdom; *perdonar las injurias es obrar como Cristianos*, to forgive injuries *is* to act like Christians.

Rule 100. The materials of which bodies are formed are denoted by *ser;* as,—*El vestido es de paño*, the suit *is* of cloth; *los candeleros son de plata*, the candlesticks *are* of silver.

Rule 101. *To be,* forming the passive voice, or used impersonally, is, generally, translated *ser;* as,—*Is* it not to be wondered at that virtue *should be* so often despised? *¿no es de maravillarse que la virtud sea tan amenudo despreciada?*

Rule 102. Possession or destination is expressed with *ser;* as,—*La corona es del rey*, the crown is the king's; *esta maquina es para copiar cartas*, this machine *is* to copy letters.

Rule 103. Locality is denoted by *estar;* as,—*El*

estaba *en la calle*, he *was* in the street; *el reo está delante del juez*, the culprit *is* before the judge.

Rule 104. *Estar* is always employed to conjugate a verb in the gerund; as,—Estoy *escribiendo*, I am writing; *hemos* estado *arguyendo*, we have *been* arguing.

Rule 105. Before adverbs or adverbial expressions denoting manner, we generally use *estar*; as,—Está *de moda*, he *is* in the fashion; estoy *de priesa*, I *am* in haste.

Rule 106. *Ser* requires the same case before as after it; as,—*Si* yo *fuera* tú, *if I* were *thou*; *si* tú *fueras* ella, if *thou* wert *she*.

Exercises on the foregoing Rules.

We *are* always merry. In truth, he *was* the most
    A *siempre alegre á la verdad*   B
graceful of all. I *am* not in that country you speak of.
ayrosa   A   *pais*
We *were* tired of marching. His presence *is* always a
   B *cansado marchar*   A
torment to me. Telemachus, come to rest, for
     para   *ven á descansar porque*
thy clothes *are* wet. If I *were* a severe judge. Who
   vestido A *mojado si*   K 1   *severo*
is thy father? I *was* then well. When the treaty
A   B *entonces bueno quando*   *tratado*
was about to [be concluded] she was ill. When
B*   *concluirse*   *malo*
kings *are* beloved, they deserve to *be so*. When madmen
     A *amado* ▲ *merecen* ▲ †   *loco*
are not raving, they *are* less objects of fear than of
A   *furioso*   A   *temor*
diversion. This woman *was* one of those who have
               B   *no tienen*

---

* See Observation after Rule 106, Grammar.
† See note *a*, to Rule 106, Grammar.

nothing reserved; she *was* [well off], *being* the wife of an
　　　　　　　　　　B　　　　　　　bien　　R　A
officer who *was* with the army. Our conversation *was*
　　　　　　　B　　　　　　　　　　　　　　　　　　　　　C
interrupted　by his entrance, and [after having] been
interrumpido con　　*entrada*　　*despues de haber*
interrupted　two hours, I took up the discourse and said
interrumpido　　　　*tomé* A　　*palabra*　　　　*dixe*
thus. They repaired to where Domingo and I *were*. If
　　　　acudieron adonde　　　　　　　　　　　B
asi
　slavery　is miserable, sovereignty is no less *so*. They
esclavitud A　　　　　　　*soberania*
exhorted　me to *be* in good humour. He loved me as
exhortaron　á P *de bueno humor*　　*amaba*　*como*
if I *had been* his son. Our voices *were* not very pleasing.
　　M 1　　　　　　　　　　　　B　　　　　*grato*
Envy　*is* the torment of the envious. Thou *art* among
embidia A　　　　　　　*embidioso*　　A　　*entre*
men what I *am* among women; this *is* the greatest praise
　　　　　A　　　　　　　　　　　A　　　　*alabanza*
which I can give thee. The Lyceum *was* at Athens, and
　　　　puedo dar　　　　*Liceo*　B *en Atenas*
was the public school. Here *is* my purse; it *is* rather
　B　　　*escuela aqui* A　　*bolsa*　　A *un poco*
empty, but thou knowest that a poor singer *is* not a bishop.
vacio pero　　　*sabes que*　　　　*cantor* A　　*obispo*
All the houses are already　let,　because they are
　　　　　　　　　　　　　ya　alquilado porque
always let [at the beginning] of the year. I *am*
　　　　　　á *principios*　　　　　　　　　　　　A
expecting some gentlemen of consequence. The bridge
esperando　　*caballero*　　*importancia*　　*puente*
was of marble, but the railings *were* of iron. I *was*
　B　*mármol*　　　*barandilla* B　*hierro*　　　B
counting my money. My greatest embarrassment *is*,
contando　*dinero*　　　　　　　　　*embarazo*　A
that I *am* far from that town. Vulcan *was* lame.
que　A *lejos*　　　*ciudad*　*Vulcano* B　*coxo*

ON SER AND ESTAR. 73

The hundred gates of the city of Babylon *were* of
      puerta   ciudad   Babilonia   B
brass. I *am* not yet his, replied the daughter. Either
bronze   A   aun   replicó   O
he really *is* a fool, or he *was* then drunk, and [I had
     A   tonto ó   B   entónces borracho
a great mind to] tell him so. The documents [*were*
†   decir   *   documento   B †
not yet] signed. To comfort the afflicted *is* an act of
   firmar   ▲ consolar á afligido A   obra
mercy. Eternity is a continued circle; its centre *is*
misericordia eternidad   uno continuo círculo   centro
[every where], but its circumference [no where]. It
en todas partes pero   circunferencia en ninguna
is certain that war *is* sometimes necessary; but it *is*
A cierto   guerra A   necesario   A
not always so. The more a man *is* elevated, the less he
            A elevado
ought *to be* proud. An obedient son *is* the comfort of
debe   P   A   consuelo
his parents. Ambitious men *are* never satisfied. Who-
        A   contento
ever wishes *to be* good may *be* so. This garden *is* in
   desee   P   puede P   A
good order, but the walks *are* too narrow. An affront
       calle f. A   angosto   afrenta
is an imaginary evil. Time seems very short to him who
A   daño   parece
is always well employed. We ought often to reflect that
A   ocupado
Death perhaps *is* not very far from us; that when we
    quizá   A
[*shall be*] in the grave it will no longer *be* time [to
  I   sepulcro   mas   F   de
repent;] that the present instant *is* all that is ours;
arrepentirse   A

---

* See Note *a*, to Rule 106, Grammar.
† See Observation after Rule 106, Grammar.

E

and that although many *are* called, few [*will be*] chosen.
                     A *llamado*   F *escogido*

On the Verbs HABER and TENER.

Rule 107. *To have*, used as an active verb, is translated *tener;* and as an auxiliary, *haber ;* as,—*I have* relations, tengo *parientes;* we *had* spoken, habiamos *hablado*.

We had given them all that we had. They had no
  B *dado*   *lo que*   B   B
other riches. All that man has, he has received from
                     A   A   *recibido*
God. If we had told her who had the letter which she
            M 1 *dicho*   B
had written, she would have doubted it. Had they had
B *escrito*   M 1 *dudado*   M 2
reason to complain, we would not have blamed them.
   de quexarse   M 3 *culpado*

Observation.—Adam was nine hundred and thirty years
             Adan B
old when he died. Although Tantalus has the water
   quando murió aunque Tántalo A
close to his lips, he always is thirsty. Women and chil-
junto á   A
dren are afraid of spectres. Some persons endeavour to
  A   *á espectro*   *se empeñan en*
appear wicked, only because they are ashamed of being
parecer malo solo porque   A   P
good. The water has not been so cold this winter as it
               D
was [last winter], and consequently we have not been
C *el hibierno pasado*
so cold.

Rule 108. When the auxiliaries *to have* and *to*

be, followed by an infinitive, denote some future action, the former is translated *tener que*, and the latter *haber de;* as,—We had to write, *teniamos que escribir;* he was to come, *habia de venir*.

Who fears God has nothing to fear. He had lived
    teme á A   *temer* B *vivido*
as if he had not a soul to save, or was never to
      K 1   *salvar* K 3 *nunca*
die. Here we are to sleep, said one of the horsemen.
morir   A *dormir dixo*   *caballero*
We had many letters to write that night, because the
  B   *escribir*
ship was to sail the next day.
navio B *salir* *siguiente*

Note a.—There was much to fear from such a
         A   B   *temer*   *tal* A
meeting. There [will be] many obstacles to overcome.
encuentro A   F   *vencer*

ETYMOLOGICAL EXERCISES ON VERBS.

On the Regular Verbs.*

Infinitives ending in *ar* are of the first, in *er* of the second, and in *ir* of the third conjugation.

First Conjugation.*

The dog barks when we knock at the door.
  perro ladrar A   *llamar* A *á*
The horses [did neigh]. The bulls bellowed. The
    relinchar B   *toro bramar* C
sheep have bleated. The cats had mewed. The asses
oveja *balar* D   *gato* *maullar* E   *asno*

* See Grammar, p. 57.

will   bray.   The   wild   boars will   have   grunted.
   rebuznar F   *jabalí*   *arruar* G
[Howl, ye] wolves! Though doves may coo. If
ahullar H   *lobo*   *aunque paloma*   *arrullar* I
  serpents [were not to hiss], though hens might
serpientes f.   *silbar* K 1   *gallina*
     cluck,   chickens would pule.   Though they may
cacarear K 2 *pollo*   *piar* K 3
arrive   before thy return.   Unless   the geese have
llegar 1* *ántes de*   *vuelta á ménos que*   *ansar*
not cackled. If the cocks had not crowed so early,
   graznar L   *gallo*   *cantar* M 1 *temprano*
the hens would not have chuckled. If the mice should
                          coclear M 3   *raton*
squeak, or the bees should have hummed.
chillar N   *abeja*   *zumbar* O

Second Conjugation.†

I fear his vengeance. We shall have dined at
  temer A   *venganza*   *comer* G
four o'clock. Thou didst owe a large sum. They
                        deber B *grande cantidad*
will corrupt thy morals.   He read the book with
    corromper F   *costumbre* f.   ‡ *leer* C
attention. Let them conquer with their words. We
                 § *vencer* H
have   lost   his friendship. Although the minister may
     perder D
possess the confidence of the prince. We would not
poseer I   *confianza*
offend   them. If they should have drunk that liquor.
ofender K 3   *beber* O   *licor*
If thou hadst gathered the flowers. If ye granted
            coger M 1   *conceder* K 2
them the favour, they would correspond with grati-
             gracia   *corresponder* K 3

* See Grammar, p. 144.   † Ibid. p. 60.
‡ See N.B. Grammar, p. 143. § See Observation, Grammar, p. 144.

ON VERBS.

tude. Although he may have committed the crime. If
          cometer L
they should eat this fruit If her poverty had not
   comer N *fruta*   *pobreza*
proceeded from her extravagance, I would have pro-
proceder M 2   *pro-*
tected her, because she had not offended me.
teger M 3   E

Third Conjugation.*

The king prohibited the export of silk goods. I shall
   prohibir C *extraccion seda género*
have set out before thy return. We have often
  partir G
applied to him. I do not permit his visits. Let us
acudir D á   *permitir* A
restrain his ambition. If hogs were not to grunt,
restriñir H   *puerco*   *gruñir* K 1
though lions might roar, they would not stun
   leon *rugir* K 2   *aturdir* K 3
me. Thou didst always elude our vigilance. Though
        eludir B
they may feign their grief. Ye had exacted [too
  †*fingir* I *pena*   *exîgir* E de-
much]. If this general should direct his operations
masiado   *dirigir* N
well. Provided the allies have fought with equal forces.
   con tal que *aliado* *combatir* L *igual*
If they should have omitted the date. If they had not
     omitir O *fecha*
lived together, they would not have quarrelled so
vivir M 1 *juntos*   *reñir* M 3
often.

* See Grammar, page 63.
† See Observation, Grammar, page 144.

On Verbs conjugated as Passive.*

I was taken prisoner in that battle. The law had
      tomar C *prisionero*
been annulled by the parliament. The victory would have
anular E
been gained by us, if our troops had not been twice
conseguir M 1 *por*   *tropa*
repulsed. Was not the castle [given up] before
rechazar M 2   *entregar* C *ántes que*
the guns were fired? Were the deserters shot?
cañon   *disparar* K 2   *desertor arcabucear* C
Many are called, but few will be chosen. Should we
    llamar A   *escoger* F
not have been banished, if we had been accused?
         desterrar M 1   *acusar* M 2
†The importation had been forbidden. †The news of
     entrada   *prohibir* E   *noticia*
the defeat was spread now and then. †The
   derrota   *esparcir* B *de quando en quando*
light of Revelation never [will be extinguished],
luz   ————   *nunca*   *apagar* F
notwithstanding all the efforts of incredulity.
no obstante   *esfuerzo*   *incredulidad*

On Verbs conjugated as Reflective.‡

I always avail myself of the opportunity. Let
     aprovecharse A   *ocasion*
men accustom themselves to labour. They com-
   acostumbrarse H   *trabajo*   *que-*
plained continually of the abuses. If thou wert to
xarse B *continuamente*   *abuso*
amuse thyself with me. If the Lord Mayor had
divertirse K 2   .   *Regidor*
not exerted himself so much, the bread [would
    empeñarse M 1

---

* See Grammar, p. 67.   † Ibid. p. 145.   ‡ Ibid. p. 71.

have become dearer]. We have flattered ourselves
encarecerse M 3 *mas*   *lisonjearse* D
too much. I shall apply myself to logic. Provided
          aplicarse F   *Con tal que*
we might free ourselves from his dominion. Had ye
     librarse K 2   *dominacion*
not deceived yourselves many times! If the government
     engañarse E
should have seized upon his papers. Let us rejoice
       apoderarse O *de*   *regocijarse* H
at the victory.
de

On the Irregular Verbs.*

I. I hate flattery. [In order] that we may not
    aborrecer A *lisonja*   *afin de que*
want his protection. Provided that the judge
carecer de I   *con tal que*
should pity her tears. Let them all suffer
   compadecerse de N   *padecer* H
the punishment, though only one may deserve it.
   castigo   *merecer* I
[In order] that cruelty may not tarnish the brilliancy of
á fin de   *deslucir* I   *esplendor*
the victory.

II. Many shut their ears to the voice of conscience.
     cerrar A   *oido*
Though they may cross the river. In order that
         atravesar I
they may defend the place. Let him govern with
    defender I   *plaza*   *gobernar* H
wisdom. They err unwillingly.
       †*errar* A *de mala gana*

III. Let them substitute another in my place.
      substituir H   *lugar*
Though he may argue with me. I contribute some-
   argüir   *contribuir* A

---

* See their Examples, Grammar, page 147.
† See Grammar, page 181.

times. Thou attributest the victory to chance. They
     atribuir A   *suerte* f.
distribute their property among the poor.
distribuir A *caudal* *entre*
 V. Let them review the works with impartiality. We
    rever H *obra* *imparcialidad*
did not then foresee our misfortunes. I foresee
  entónces prever B *desgracia* *antever* A
the consequences of this disagreement. They never have
       desavenencia
reviewed that pamphlet.
rever D *folleto*
 VII. Though the authority may decay. In order that
       decaer I
we may not relapse into the same habits. Provided the
   recaer I *mismo hábito*
responsibility should not devolve upon me.
responsabilidad *recaer* I
 VIII. I hear his voice. From that place they hear
   oir A   *desde* *sitio* A
every thing with ease. In order that he [may not
    facilidad
hear indistinctly] the conversation. Let them overhear
 entreoir I   *entreoir* H
all the conference.
 IX. [I am ashamed] of his conduct. Let my tears
  avergonzarse A
move thee. [He lays bets] sometimes. He returns, that
mover H *apostar* A   *volver* A
they may absolve him. Smell that rose. Though the
 absolver I **oler* H *rosa*
altar may smell of the incense. Cost what it cost.
altar *oler* I *á* *incienso costar* H I
 X. He contends with me. Correct her. In order
   competir A *corregir* H
that we may obtain our pretensions. Let us dismiss
   †*conseguir* I   *despedir* H

   * See Grammar, page 183.
   † See Observation, Grammar, page 144.

them immediately. Measuring their forces with ours.
       medir R
If the fire should melt the wax. Though they may
  fuego *derretir* N *cera*
ask alms. Provided they do not quarrel.
pedir I *limosna*   *reñir* I

  XI. He acquires the esteem of his countrymen.
     adquirir A
Warn them of the danger. Defer not thy conver-
advertir H   *peligro* *deferir* I
sion until old age. Adhering always to the same
 hasta vejez *adherir* R
opinion. In order that we might consent to it. If
dictámen   *consentir* K 2 *en*
thou shouldst confer with him upon the subject.
   conferir N *sobre asunto*

  XII. He died the following year. Die with
    morir C *siguiente* *morirse* H *de*
shame. Let us die the death of the righteous. Al-
   morir H   *justo*
though he might die of grief. He [is dying] for
   morir K 2   *morirse* A *por*
her. If he should die of this illness. Dying
    morir N *enfermedad morir* R
for his country.
 patria

  XVI. I satisfy him with little. He counterfeited
   satisfacer A   *contrahacer* C
the coin of the realm. If they should not do
moneda *reyno*
over again what we have undone. Satisfy him. If
rehacer N   *deshacer* D *satisfacer* H
they were to undo it, we would do it over again.
   K 1   K 3

  XIX. Let us suppose it. We would never oppose
    suponer H   *oponerse á* K 3
a negotiation. Let them propose the conditions.
      proponer H

[Make thyself acquainted] with their proposals. They
 imponerse H   *en*   *propuesta*
will presuppose our consent. I prefer virtue
 presuponer F *consentimiento* *anteponer* A
to riches. They have composed various works. If
       componer D
they should expose her to his rage. Ye deposed the
   exponer N *cólera* *deponer* C
sovereign.

 XXII. Her groans attracted the attention of the
     gemido *atraer* C
hearers. Although they may contract many debts.
oyente   *contraer* I *deuda*
To the end that the delinquents [might take refuge] in
          retraerse K 2
the church. Let them subtract the half of the quantity.
     subtraer H *mitad*

 XXIII. Although it may not be worth the while.
         valer I *pena*
The profits would never be equivalent to the labour.
ganancia   *equivaler* K 3 *trabajo*
I do not go out early. He will surpass his predecessors
 salir A   *sobresalir á* F
in humility. Surpass thy ancestors in virtue.
 sobresalir á H *antepasados*

 XXIV. The innkeeper conducted me to the house of
   mesonero *conducir* C
a carrier. If this orator were never to introduce
arriero   *introducir* K I
his similes. Though he may not seduce her with his pro-
——   *seducir* I   *pro-*
mises. If the trees should not produce fruit [next
mesa *árbol*   *producir* N *el verano*
summer]. Provided we translate the documents.
que viene   *traducir* I *documento*

 XXVI. We shall abide by your opinion. Let us
    atenerse F *á*
not detain her. In order that they might [keep up]
 detener I   *mantener* K 2

their establishment. He would not entertain them.
establecimiento   *entretener* K 3
Restrain thy passions. If they should not abstain
contener H   *abstenerse* N
from strong liquors.
fuerte licor

XXVII. Let them agree better in future. Though
              avenirse H   *en adelante*
some accident may happen to them, they never will
                        sobrevenir I
infringe the laws. The bad smell arose from the
contravenir á F   *mal olor provenir* C
drain. But if a verb should intervene. We pre-
caño   pero   intervenir N
pared ourselves for the battle.
prevenirse C

XXVIII. I never retract what I have said. They
              desdecirse de   D
will bless the hand. He had predicted that they
     bendecir F   *predecir* E
would curse him. Though he should contradict
       maldecir K 3   *contradecir* N
the assertion, I will not retract. If they should curse
afirmacion   F   N
us in their wrath. If they had blessed them. This bread
     enojo   M 1*
is blessed.
T*

On the Impersonal Verbs.†

Amanecer, Anochecer, Nevar, Helar, &c.

It will not be light so soon to-morrow. It snowed
         amanecer F *temprano mañana*   *nevar* C
two hours after it was dark. Though it may grow dark
                anochecer C   *anochecer* I

* See Observation, Grammar, page 188.
† See Grammar, page 188 to 193.
‡ See Observation, Grammar, page 246.

early. If it should thunder and lighten, we shall see
             tronar N   relampaguear N   ver F
the road by the flashes of lightning. Though it may
  camino á   luz   relámpagos
thunder and lighten to-night, we [shall be at break
    I   I   esta noche   amanecer F
of day] with the army.
                exército

Haber.

There are some unhappy moments in which the most
         A   desgraciado   qual
virtuous are the most feeble. There is no government in
virtuoso   débil   A
which there have not been some variations. Provided
              L   mudanza
there be honour, there will be security. There would
    I   honra   F seguridad
have been many disputes, though certainly there was
M I   á la verdad   B
no cause. Then said the Creator, Let there be light;
                                             H
and there was light.
        C

Hacer.

It is cold; but provided it should be no colder than
 A frio pero   I
it has been to-day, it will not be so cold this winter as it
   D   hoy   F   invierno
was last winter. It was then ten years since they
 C   B entónces   que
[had written to us]. It is more than a hundred years
 no nos escribian   A
since they rebuilt the church of Saint Paul. On the
           reedificar C iglesia San Pablo A
sixth of February it will be eight years since he came here.
    F   que   acá

On the Observation, Grammar, p. 193.

There needs no more than a bad inclination to make
  no ser menester A   ——— *para hacer á*
a man vicious. It is not enough to think with exactness,
  vicioso   *bastar* A   *pensar*   *exâctitud*
we must also express ourselves with clearness. It
ser menester A *expresarse*   *claridad*
is necessary to prefer our duty to our pleasure. It
ser preciso A *preferir*   *obligacion*   *gusto*
is not enough for a general to be prudent, it is also
    bastar A
necessary that he be fortunate. It is the Gospel that
       afortunado   *evangelio*
commands us to forgive our enemies. It is not those
manda   *perdonar* á
who speak most that men admire. It is thou who
hablar A *mas*   *admirar* A
hast deceived us. Men must obey the laws, since
engañar D   *ser menester* A   *puesque*
it is they that defend us.
    defender A

On the Use of the Tenses.*

Present and Imperfect of the Indicative.

God is propitious to those who implore him. Nero
    propicio   *implorar*
was a detestable tyrant. All men talk of liberty, savages
                 hablar   *salvage*
alone possess it. The Lacedemonians sacrificed their
solo poseer   *Lacedemonio sacrificar á*
children. He sets out to-morrow for Spain. The pro-
 hijo   *partir*   *para*   *pró-*
digal lives rich and dies poor, the miser lives poor and
digo vivir   *morir*   *avaro*
dies rich. Most people live without reflection.

* See Grammar, from page 195 to 215.

On the Perfect Indefinite, Perfect Definite, and Pluperfect.

God has imprinted in the heart of man the love of
     estampar
liberty. As soon as Cæsar had entered the senate, the
   luego que   *entrar en*
conspirators threw themselves upon him. All his honours,
    echarse   *honra*
riches, and power, vanished immediately. It is now
      vanecer   *hacer*
four years since he has been with the army. We had
      que
then corresponded with each other for more than ten
entónces *cartearse*
years. When man considers how long he has
      considerar quanto tiempo ▲
offended his Creator, and that he has pardoned him, he
ofender á   *perdonar* ▲
shudders. No sooner had Adam heard the voice of the
estremecerse no bien   *oir*
Lord than he [grew ashamed].
 quando *avergonzarse*

On the Future Imperfect and the Future Perfect.

The prayers of the righteous will be efficacious. I
 oracion   *justo*   *eficaz*
shall set off to-day, and shall have spoken with him
 partir   *hablar*
before his return. God will reward the good, and
ántes de vuelta   *recompensar*
will punish the wicked. Perhaps the commissioners
 castigar *malo* ▲ *comisionado*
are now signing the capitulation. I suppose you have
   firmando ——— ▲
read the Gazette. Is there a grief like mine? Some
leer

said, Can this man be a Deity under the human form?
decir   deidad baxo   figura
The world will have existed next year* five thousand eight
hundred and thirty-three years.

On the Imperative and the Present of the Subjunctive.

Come to see me to-morrow, daughter, but come not
venir
early. Let us profit by his example. Forgive them
           aprovecharse   perdonar
Father, for they know not what they do. Use thy
                saber   hacer usar de
authority with moderation, and do not abuse thy power.
autoridad   abusar de poder
Remember, man, that thou art dust.
 acordarse   polvo

On the Terminations RA, SE, and RIA.†

How many men would have perished in that battle!
     quanto   perecer
Nations would be happy, if wisdom were the only object
              feliz   sabiduria   único
of sovereigns. Had we no pride, we should not complain
                                                quexarse
of the pride of others. We should be happy now, if
Adam had not sinned. Caligula commanded that the
            pecar   mandar
Romans should render him divine honours. Were men
              tributar
to follow always the dictates of reason, [they would save
   seguir   precepto
themselves] many sorrows. Had Cæsar been less am-
ahorrarse
bitious, he would have honoured human nature more.
                              honrar

* 1829   † See Grammar, page 209.

Did you but know, brother, where I am now, you would
         saber
put up a thousand supplications to heaven, that I might
ofrecer   *súplica*   *porque*
return to your house. Oh! [had I but seen] her before
volver   *o*   *ver*
her death! He ordered the general to take the fortress,
      mandar   *tomar fortaleza*
and to [put to death as many as] he found armed, and
y que matar á quantos encontrar armado
to pay for all the provisions which he might want.
que pagar   *víveres*   *necesitar*
Without temptations we should not be able to know
            poder conocerse
ourselves. The innkeeper to whom I related my adven-
yo mismo *posadero*   *contar* *aven-*
ture, (with which the scoundrel was perhaps better
tura de el qual bellaco estar* quizá
acquainted than I,) pitied me. We had written
informado   *compadecerse de*
to know if the vessel [would set sail] the following
para saber si *navio hacerse á la vela*
week.

On the different Significations of the Preterimperfect and Imperfect Future of the Subjunctive.

No one seemed to me, then, more suited to believe
    parecer   *entónces* *apto para creer*
every thing I might choose to tell him. Thou wilt have
todo   *querer decir*
[as many conveniences as] [thou mayest choose]. He
quantas conveniencias   *querer*
gave them permission to do what [they might happen to
        de hacer   *querer*
like]; hence it is that they did then what they chose;
  de aquí   *querer*

* See the last N.B. Grammar, page 211.

they do now what they choose; and doubtless will do
                       querer   *sin duda*
hereafter what they will. Ye may stop in my her-
en adelante   *querer*   *poder quedarse   her-*
mitage [as long as] ye like. [We shall march] on the
mita todo el tiempo que querer   marcharémos
twelfth, and he that has valour on that day let him then
                                                    entónces
follow me. If I were a king I would do what I like.
seguir   *hacer*
He had ordered that all neutral vessels which should
         mandar   *neutral buque*
  enter   the ports of England, or should have been
entrar en   puerto
searched by the English cruisers, should be confiscated
registrar por   *crucero*   *confiscar*
[as soon as] they entered the ports of France.
luego que

SYNTACTICAL EXERCISES ON VERBS.

On the Agreement of the Verb with its Subject.

Rule 109. The verb and its subject agree in number and person; as,—*El maestro enseña, y los discípulos aprenden,* the master teaches, and the scholars learn.

Fortune and caprice govern the world. A babbler
            capricho gobernar   *hablador*
speaks when we do not listen to him, and does not
hablar quando   *escuchar*
listen to us when we speak to him. Interest and vanity occasion the greatest portion of human misery.
causar   *parte f.*

Rule 110. If the subject of the verb be a collective noun, the verb may be put in the plural; as,—

Una multitud entráron, a multitude entered. See also note *a.*

An infinity of persons came to offer me their services.
infinidad sujeto venir á ofrecer atencion
A multitude gnawed his entrails. The majority
muchedumbre f. *roer entraña pluralidad*
opposed the resolutions. The parliament decreed that
oponerse á parlamento decretar
the army [should return].
exército volver

Rule 111. A verb having different persons for its subjects, agrees with the pronoun understood; as,— *El rey y la reyna* (ellos) *entraron,* the king and queen (*they*) came in.

Thou and he who conducts thee shall perish. As soon
          guiar perecer luego
as we saw our master dead, Dame Jacinta Inesilla and
que amo muerto Señora
I began a concert of mournful howlings. Her father
comenzar música fúnebre alarid
and mother [will not consent].
      consentir

Rule 112. If a verb has several subjects not connected by a conjunction, it agrees generally with the last; as,—*Esquadras, exércitos, dinero, todo se sacrificó,* fleets, armies, money, all was sacrificed.

Wealth, dignities, honours, every thing disappears at
bienes dignidad honra desaparecer
the hour of death; virtue alone remains. Our ships,
              solo permanecer navio
our colonies, our commerce, every thing is ruined.
colonia comércio estar perdido
Games, conversation, spectacles, nothing amuses her.
uego espectáculo divertir

Note a.—Not only his property and his health, but
        solamente   *caudal*   *salud sino*
his reputation also has been sacrificed. The heavens,
———— *tambien*   *sacrificar*   *cielo*
the earth, and even man, show his omnipotence.
tierra   *aun*   *manifestar* *omnipotencia*

Note b.—(5) His valour and his constancy (2) were
            valor   *constancia*
(1) never (3) more (4) exposed, than in the last battle.
             exponer
Let (2) him and his relations (1) quit this country.
        pariente *salir de* *pais*

Observation.—I do not like to give my estate to a
              gustar dar *hacienda*
spendthrift. We will like to see the public buildings.
pródigo   *ver*   *público edificio*
The apartment could hold a bed, a press and two chairs.
aposento *caber cama armario* *silla*
The conversation of those who like to show their supe-
                      gustar mostrar supe-
riority is irksome. The Japanese have a copper idol,
rioridad enfadoso   *Japones*   *cobre*
whose head [can hold] fifteen men.
        caber

Government of Verbs

Rule 113. An active transitive verb governs the noun to which its energy passes, in the objective case; as,—*El la mató*, he killed her.

God wisely governs the world. Riches often pro-
   sabiamente gobernar   *pro-*
cure us envy. Discord always produces quarrels.
curar   *discórdia*   *contienda*
Neither riches nor dignities render us happy.
 ni   *dignidad hacer*

SYNTACTICAL EXERCISES

Rule 114. Active verbs govern their objective case with the preposition *á*, if it is a person; as—*Venció al enemigo,* he conquered the enemy.

Though [we may be able] to deceive men, we shall
        poder   Á *engañar*
never be able to deceive God. Nature makes the poet;
                                          hacer
art the orator. Minos loved his people more than his
   orador   *pueblo*
own family.
propio

    Observation.—Covetousness often begets   prodigality,
                     avaricia   *engendrar prodigalidad*
and prodigality sometimes begets covetousness. Flatterers
                                                     lisonjero
make cowards vain, and fools mad. Hope is the only
hacer cobarde vano   *necio loco esperanza*   *único*
comfort which never abandons the gamester. Philip
consuelo   *abandonar*   *jugador*   *Felipe*
sent the deputies to the minister. [Waiting for] this
mandar *diputado*   *esperar*
maturity, I did not learn to read or to write.
madurez f.   *aprender á leer ni*   *escribir*

Rule 115. Passive verbs require the preposition *de* or *por* before the noun which denotes the agent; as,—*Dios es temido de* or *por los malos,* God is feared by the wicked; *El reo fué sentenciado por el juez,* the culprit was sentenced by the judge.

An affable man is beloved by all the world. Great
    afable   *amar*
men are persecuted by envy. Learning and virtue are
        perseguir   *envidia* *ciencia*
sought by few.

    Note a.—Abel was slain by Cain. The History of

ON VERBS.

Don Quixote was written by Cervantes. The school was
               escribir
founded by them.
fundar

Rule 116. Neuter verbs active intransitive, as well as some reflective verbs, have a regimen with *de*, which denotes what causes their effects; as,—*Bramar de corage*, to roar with passion; *Correrse de la pregunta*, to blush at the question; *Me alegro de verte*, I am glad to see thee.

My grandfather wept with joy. My parents wondered at my prodigious memory. Ah! poor Gil Blas.
abuelo llorar   *padre maravillarse prodigioso memoria*
die with shame. Lucinda retired, crying with passion. I am ashamed to see thee in such a condition.
morirse vergüenza   retirarse llorando cólera avergonzarse ver   tal A ———
I soon [grew tired] of living among those wretches.
presto cansarse vivir   miserable

Note b.—We regretted much not [being able] to
             pesar   *poder*
accompany her.
acompañar

Rule 117. Verbs implying motion to, towards, or from, a place, govern the noun denoting whence the motion proceeds with *de*, the noun which points out its direction with *á*, and the noun expressing the space through which it passes with *por*; example,—*Fueron de Lóndres á Chelsea, por el Parque*, they went from London to Chelsea, through the Park.

Men often pass from love to ambition, but seldom
       pasar   ———   *rara vez*
from ambition to love. [Before we rush] upon danger,
——— ——   *ántes de arrojarnos*

94   SYNTACTICAL EXERCISES

we ought to foresee the consequences. We had then
  deber   prever   conseqüencia
passed from the hardships of slavery to the sweets of
              rigor   esclavitud   dulzura
liberty. No mortal can [go out] of this world without
libertad   ——— poder salir
passing through the gates of death.
pasar

    Observation.—I set off immediately to discharge my
                    partir al punto   executar
commission. The innkeeper came out to receive me
comision   mesonero   salir   recibir
with much urbanity. [I must go] and [look for]
        urbanidad es menester que vaya   buscar
them. He will not see her again. He again read the
                    ver   leer
paper with much attention.

    Rule 118. Verbs of *demanding*, and of *granting* or *refusing*, generally govern the person to whom their energy is directed with the preposition *á*; as,—*Pide perdon* á Dios, ask pardon *from* God.

    This wonderful secret which nature could not conceal
      maravilloso secreto   poder   ocultar
from my profound observation. We plucked from each
    profundo observacion   arrancarse
other a handful of hairs. I bought her watch of a famous
    puñado cabello   comprar   relox   famoso
watchmaker. I asked the innkeeper if he had any
reloxero   preguntar mesonero   alguno
fish. The adventures of Gil Blas, says Father Isla,
pezcado   aventura   —— ——
were stolen from Spain, and adopted in France.
      robar   adoptar

    Note a.—He made war upon the two sovereigns, and
              hacer   á

took from them various places. They always ask
tomar   *plaza*   *pedir*
leave of him, but he never grants it to them.
permision   *conceder*

Note c.—I [went out] of Ithaca to inquire after my
          salir   —   *preguntar*
father of the other kings who had returned from the siege
                               volver   *sitio*
of Troy.
Troya

Rule 119. Verbs implying *yielding*, or *resistance*, generally require *á* before the regimen to which their energy is directed; as,—*Aunque declare ella su parecer*, yo no soy uno de los que someten su opinion* al dictámen* de otros,* Although she may declare her opinion, I am not one of those who submit their opinion to the opinion of others.

No one can resist his arguments. [He has always
        poder resistir   *argumento*   *siempre*
regulated himself] by the will of his superiors. An
arreglarse   *voluntad*   *superior*
Arab who dedicates himself to the occupation of a land
Arabe   *dedicarse*   —   *tierra*
pirate, habituates himself to bear the fatigue of journeys,
pirata   *habituarse*   *sufrir*   *viage*
and accustoms himself not to sleep, and to endure heat
      hacerse   *dormir*   *tolerar calor*
and thirst.
sed

Rule 120. Verbs of *comparing* generally require *á* before the noun with which the comparison is made; as,—*El hijo se parece* al padre, the son resembles *the father.*

Those vices which resemble virtues are the worst of
                  semejarse

* See the Author's Synonyms, page 177.

all. [As for me.] I prefer my country to the
    por lo que toca á mí   *preferir*   *patria*
hundred cities of Crete. The splendour of the fortune
          Creta   *esplendor*
of the wicked resembles the lightning which precedes
    malo   *semejarse*   *relámpago*   *precede*
the [clap of thunder].
    trueno

Rule 121. Verbs implying *to belong, to concern, to happen, to play, to suit*, as well as most of the impersonal verbs, generally require *á* before the noun to which their energy is directed; as, *Importa á los Cristianos*, it concerns *Christians*.

I knew the cards, and I played at dice. It concerns
conocer   *naype*   *jugar*   *dado*   *importar*
princes to judge of their ministers, but it concerns us to
     A *juzgar*   A
submit to their will. It concerns them to consider
someterse   *considerar*
my resolution, and it concerns him to execute it. I
                                      executar
grew fond of wine.
aficionarse

Rule 122. Verbs of *condemning* require the punishment to be preceded by the preposition *á*; as,—*Condenarán al reo á galeras*, they will condemn the culprit *to the galleys*; *Sentenciaron al desertor á ser arcabuceado*, they sentenced the deserter *to be shot*.

Adam was condemned to cultivate the ground. Tan-
Adan   *condenar*   *cultivar*   *tierra*   *Tan-*
talus was condemned to a continual thirst, and to have
talo   *sed* f.
the water [up to] his chin, and [not to be able] to taste it.
      hasta   *barba*   *no poder*   A *probar*

Rule 123. Verbs implying *plenty* or *want, remembrance* or *oblivion*, have a regimen generally pre ceded by *de;* as,—*Llenó la casa* de gente, he filled the house *with people; Acuérdate* de tu Criador, remember *thy Creator.*

Remember the shortness of life, and the certainty
acordarse   brevedad   certidumbre f.
of death. Rules always need examples. Let us arm
                        necesitar   armarse
ourselves with patience. I did not doubt the death
            paciencia   dudar
of my husband. Remember that I have intrusted to thee
                    acordarse   confiar
the secret.

Rule 124. Verbs implying *praising, blaming, absolving, using, repenting, jeering,* and *pitying,* generally have a regimen also with *de;* as,—*Por la noche nos juntabamos, y nos reíamos* de *los que se habían compadecido* de *nosotros por el día,* at night we met, and used to laugh at those who had pitied us in the course of the day.

Perhaps Hazael will pity my youth and my
quizá   compadecerse
tears. The worldly will deride us; but what will not
lágrima   mundano   burlarse   pero
the worldly deride? Let us avail ourselves of
                                aprovecharse
the present time. An honest man values himself upon
                        honrado   preciarse
nothing.

Note a.—Thy parents will repent to have so much
                        arrepentirse
lectured a simpleton. We did not laugh at hearing
arengar   mentecato   reirse   oir
her sing; but at seeing her dance.
    cantar sino   ver   baylar

Rule 125. Verbs implying *distance* or *separation,* generally require *de* before the noun which is not their own direct regimen; as,—*Apártate* de la ocasion, avoid *the opportunity*.

They have degenerated from their first state. I shall
                      degenerar
mistrust myself as my most terrible enemy. I did not
desconfiar mí mismo
know him at first, because he had changed his dress.
conocer   *al principio porque*   *mudar*   *trage*
We renounce more easily our interests than our
    renunciar   *fácilmente*
pleasures.

Rule 126. Most verbs admit a regimen with *en*, denoting wherein the meaning of the said verbs is conspicuous; as,—*Siempre pensaré* en tí, I shall always think *on thee*.

We ought to think frequently on the shortness of
          pensar con freqüencia
life, and on the certainty of death. I thought only
        certidumbre f.   *pensar*
on cultivating my talent, and on applying myself to
  cultivar   *aplicarse*
labour. It is better not to abound with riches, than to
trabajo   *abundar*
burn with the desires which they excite.
abrasarse   *deseo*   *excitar*

Rule 127. Verbs denoting *behaviour*, generally require *con* before the persons towards whom it is directed; as,—*Me desahogaré* con mi padre, I will unbosom myself *to my father*.

We ought to behave well to those who have behaved
    deber   *portarse*
well to us. She plays him the same part which he
          representar   *mismo papel*
[used to play] to her. [Acquit thyself] towards thy
                             cumplir

neighbour, as thou wouldst that thy neighbour should
próximo como   querer
acquit himself towards thee.

Observation.—My mother [used to suffocate] me with
                                  sofocar
caresses. Strike him hard, said he to them, and let him
caricia   dar   recio decir
die with blows: immediately they [threw themselves]
morir   garrotazo   *echarse*
upon me, and struck me with their bludgeons. They
sobre   *garrote*
opened the breach with a single [shot of their gun].
abrir   brecha   solo   cañonazo

ON VERBAL REGIMEN.*

Rule 128. If two verbs come together in English, and the second is in the infinitive, this mood is in general likewise used in Spanish; as,—*Quiero aprender,* I wish to learn; *Debemos obedecer,* we ought to obey.

I should like to go; but he will not like to return
      querer á *ir pero*   á *volver*
with me. We ought to suffer with resignation all the
           deber á *sufrir*
evils which we cannot avoid. Men ought to flee from
mal   poder evitar   á *huir*
vice, and to practise virtue.
        á *practicar*

Rule 129. Verbs denoting *to dare, to begin, to teach, to learn, to compel,* generally require *á* before the infinitive which they govern; as,—*No me atrevo á salir,* I dare not go out.

Grammar is the art which teaches to speak and to
gramática   *enseñar*   *hablar*

* See Grammar, p. 231.

write correctly. All men ought to learn to know
escribir correctamente deber aprender conocerse
themselves. A libertine seldom begins to reform
A *libertino rara vez empezar reformarse*
[until] he [sees himself] compelled to abandon his
hasta que verse precisar abandonar
pleasures.

Rule 130. Verbs implying *to submit, to oppose, to exhort* or *invite, to prepare, to assist, to be destined,* and *to accustom one's self,* generally require *á* before the infinitive which they govern; as,—*Exhortaronme á vivir Cristianamente,* they exhorted me to live like a Christian.

I had accustomed myself to treat only with
acostumbrarse tratar únicamente
persons of distinction. Whilst they prepared to receive
persona mientras disponerse recibir
us. Religion obliges us to revere princes, and to obey
obligar reverenciar obedecer
our superiors. Help me to overcome my passions.
superior ayudar vencer pasion

Rule 131. Verbs signifying *to abstain, to cease, to deprive, to finish,* govern the infinitive with *de;* as,—*Cesaron de atormentarme,* they ceased to torment me.

I thought that fortune would cease to persecute me.
pensar que cesar perseguir
They ceased to torment me with their remedies.
atormentar remedio
I saw that I could not avoid communicating my ideas.
poder dispensarse comunicar idea

Note a.—He is just gone out. He was but just come
salir entrar
in when I saw him. She had just lost her husband.
ver perder
They have just gained a complete victory.
alcanzar

ON VERBAL REGIMEN.

Note c.—Take care not to judge the works of others.
          guardarse   *juzgar*   *obra*
I shall take care not to tell them the secret. He took
                     decir   *secreto*
good care not to return.
bien   *volver*

Note d.—It is better to prevent evil than to be under
                        mal   *á verse en*
the necessity of punishing it. He has no need to come
    precision   *castigar*   *necesidad*
so far, for I shall have time to call at his house to-day.
lejos porque   *tiempo pasar*   *hoy*

Note e.—Fortune causes (2) our virtues or vices (1) to
              hacer
be seen. He caused himself to be beloved by his subjects
ver   *hacerse*   *vasallo*
by his affability. The mayor ordered us to [be taken up].
por afabilidad corregidor mandar á *prender*
Men suffer themselves often to be overcome by tempta-
      dexarse   *vencer*
tions, because they dare not expose themselves to the
                atreverse
sarcasms of the world.
sarcasmo

Observation.—It was not easy to [meet with] a more
                         á *hallar*
favourable conjuncture to free ourselves from his do-
          conjuntura   *librarse*   *do-*
minion. To obtain a convenient seat, it was necessary
minacion   *lograr*   *cómodo asiento*
to go very early; but who [would not rise betimes] to
á   *temprano*   *madrugar*
have the pleasure of hearing his speeches? The victory
      gusto   *oir*   *discurso*
is not yet gained. The capitulation was not signed.
    alcanzar   ——   *firmar*
There remains to us [a great deal] to suffer. Nothing
  quedar   *mucho*   *padecer*

ought to be left undone. Our wrongs remain still
            hacer   *agravio*   *aun*
unrevenged.
vengar

*Regimen in the Indicative or Subjunctive.**

Rule 132. When two verbs come together in English, and the latter is governed in the indicative or subjunctive with a conjunction, the Spanish verb will in general admit the same mood; as,—*Díxóme este que* pensaba *partir temprano,* the latter told me that he *meant* to set out early.

Consider, man, that every thing has had a beginning
considerar   *principio*
and that it will have an end. I never thought that my
         fin   *nunca creer*
name would be known at Penaflor. He contrived that
        conocer en ————   *disponer*
we should be conducted to a very retired room. I ex-
       conducir   *retirado*
pected he would have come to-day.
†   *venir hoy*

Observation.—I could receive him then, and so I
      poder recibir   *entónces*   *así*
told Agnes to conduct him to my room. They ordered
decir Ines   *conducir*   *quarto*   *mandar*
him to teach me, but they permitted him only to
    enseñar   *mas*   *permitir*
threaten me. I wish to go there to-morrow, and I
amenazar   *querer* á *allá*
wish you to go with me. Joseph told his brethren to
                                          decir
return and bring Benjamin.
volver   *traer*

* See Directions for placing the Verbal Regimen in the Subjunctive, Grammar, p. 238.
† See N.B. after this Rule, Grammar.

Rule 133. Verbs denoting *fitness* or *necessity*, *command* or *permission*, *desire* or *joy*, *wonder* or *doubt*, and impersonals used interrogatively or negatively, generally have their regimen in the subjunctive; as,—*Mandó que rindiesen la plaza*, he ordered the place to be given up; *No hay ninguno que vaya*, there is no one to go.

It is not to [be wondered at] that the superstitious ages
              de maravillarse   *supersticioso siglo*
have produced an unbelieving age. There are very few
    producir   *incrédulo*
who [have not exposed themselves] to temptations. The
        exponerse   *tentacion*
judge ordered the carrier to be stripped, and that in his
    mandar   *desnudar*
presence they should give him two hundred lashes.
        dar   *azote*

Note a.—Though thou come a hundred times. [In
         venir   *á*
order] that no one [might know] it. [To the end] that
fin de   *saber*   *para*
you [may be convinced]. [Lest] thou fall into tempta-
    convencerse   *no sea que*   *caer en*
tion. Provided we put our trust in God.
  con tal que   *poner*   *confianza*

Promiscuous Exercises.

Charity is the virtue which men want most. [They
              carecer mas
have not acquitted themselves] towards her as they ought.
    cumplir   *deber*
They will not like his voice. Contradiction ought to
     gustar   *deber* á
awaken attention, and not anger. All those who
despertar atencion   *cólera*
know their temper, do not always know their heart.
conocer   *genio* á   *siempre*   *corazon*

The elders [were astonished] at my answers. Again
   anciano   *espantarse*   *respuesta.*
she sang, and again they hissed her. I mounted a
  cantar   *silvar*   *montar*
good horse, which they had taken from the gentleman.
                          coger   *caballero*
We ought to resist the temptations of the world.
  deber Á *resistir*   *tentacion*
Malice [takes pleasure] in lowering our pride. At hearing
malicia complacerse   *abatir*   á *el oir*
this she changed countenance. Men ought not to forget
     mudar semblante   *deber*   *olvidarse*
what they are, nor the end for which they were created.
              ni   *fin*
But the wise Mentor opposed so rash a design. The
pero sabio ——— *oponerse temerario designio*
father wept with joy when he saw his daughter, and the
llorar   *gozo*   *ver*
mother seemed [as if she would] [devour her] with
    parecer que queria comersela
kisses. The parents of the [young gentleman] allowed
beso   *caballerito* *dexarse*
themselves easily to be deceived. Let us behave
  Á *fácilmente*   *engañar*   *portarse*
in such a manner to all, as to deserve the esteem
de   *modo*   *merecer estimacion*
of the good. It suffices us to know that it is a work
         basta   *obra*
of his, to be persuaded that it is an excellent work.
  estar persuadido
Youth wants wisdom to deliberate, and old age power
    carecer   *vejez*
to execute.

ON THE GERUND.

Rule 134. The English participle present is construed by the gerund in Spanish; as,—The news being certain, *siendo ciertas las noticias.*

ON THE GERUND.

I have been reading, and he is now writing. Then
   leer   *escribir*
turning to her, and seeing her grief, he said. They
volverse   *ver* *aflicciou*
were coming* towards us; but having observed† our
 venir   *hácia*   *observar*
position, and believing our forces superior, they fled.
    creer   *huir*

Rule 135. Gerunds admit the same preposition before their regimen as the verbs from which they are derived; as,—*Arrepentiendose* de *sus culpas,* repenting his crimes.

Rule 136. The present participle, when used in English as a verbal noun, is resolved into the present of the infinitive in Spanish; as,—The pleasure of *speaking* to him, *el gusto de* hablarle.

The Asiatics, remembering the dignity of Berenice,
  Asiano *acordarse* *dignidad*
and pitying her hard fate, sent her succours. I
 compadecerse *malo suerte* f. *enviar* *socorro*
saw her coming,‡ and profiting by the opportunity [I
ver *venir* *aprovecharse* *ocasion*
went away] without saying a word; but she heard me
 irse   *palabra*   *oir*
[going‡ out]. Claudina looked without ceasing towards
 salir   *mirar* *cesar* *hácia*
the place. Happiness does not consist in living, but in
 sitio *felicidad* *consistir* *vivir sino en*
[knowing how] to live. At last Domingo, after
 saber   *en fin*   *despues de*
having eaten§ and drunk well, went to his stable.
 comer *beber bien*   *caballeriza*

---
* See note *b* to this Rule, Grammar.
† See Compound of the Gerund, Grammar, p. 240.
‡ See note *a*, to Rule 134, Grammar.
§ See Compound of the Gerund, Grammar, p. 240.

We took the place without having fired a gun. Clouds
tomar   plaza   disparar cañon nube f.
are formed from exhalations, arising* from the earth.
formar   levantarse
I met them marching* towards the fortress.
encontrar marchar   fortaleza

Note a.—We shall obtain peace by making great sa-
lograr   hacer
crifices. I convinced him by representing their wants;
convencer   representar   necesidad
and by [reminding] him of his former friendship.
traer á la memoria †   *antigua amistad*

ON THE PARTICIPLE.

Rule 137. The participle is indeclinable when it is employed to form the compound tenses of any verb; as,—*Nosotros le hemos* ofendido, *y él nos ha* perdonado, we have *offended* him, and he has *pardoned* us.

The armies have fought with intrepidity.
              combatir   intrepidez
[How many] have repented not having [applied them-
quanto   arrepentirse   aplicarse
selves] to study in their youth, having suffered (2) many
      estudio   juventud   dexar
opportunities (1) to escape, wherein they might have
              escapar   en que
profited by the instructions they had received!
aprovecharse   recibir

Rule 138. When the participle is not preceded by the auxiliary *haber*, it assumes all the properties of a verbal adjective, and is consequently declinable; as,—*Los justos serán* premiados, the righteous will be *rewarded; Ella parece* afligida, she seems *afflicted*.

* See Observation, Grammar, p. 240.
† See *, Grammar, p. 227.

The wicked are always tormented by their own con-
malo   *atormentar*
science. All chemical preparations, said Doctor San-
         químico   *decir*
grado, appear to me invented to ruin nature. Let
     parecer   *idear*   *arruinar*
us consider who has given us being, and for what end
    considerar   *dar*   *ser*   *para que*
we have been created; how many are the mercies
          crear   *gracia*
received; and how great the ingratitude with which we
recibir
have repaid them
    pagar

Note a.—I have written to him four letters on the
          tener escribir
subject, but he has not replied to any. I had
asunto   *tener*   *contestar*   *ninguna*   *tener*
spoken to them, and had convinced them. [He concealed
hablar   *tener convencer*   *ocultarse*
himself] to avoid the praises which he had so well
        evitar   *alabanza*   *tener*
deserved.
merecer

Note b.—This ceremony being concluded, they put
         ceremonia   *concluir*   *poner*
me at the door. The male issue of the Gothic kings
        puerta   *masculino línea*   *godo*
being extinct, the crown of Leon passed to his sister.
    extinguir   —— *pasar*
The rebels being vanquished, the army returned to
    rebelde   *vencer*   *volver*
England. Having obtained the king's license, we set off
               conseguir   *partir*
immediately.
 al punto

ON ADVERBS.*

Rule 139. When two or more adjectives are to be formed into adverbs, to modify the same verb, the adverbial termination is added to the last adjective only; as,—*Habla clara y concisamente,* he speaks clearly and concisely.

He composes correctly, writes elegantly, and speaks
componer correcto escribir elegante hablar
eloquently. A friend who candidly and judiciously
eloqüente cándido juicioso
warns us secretly of our faults, is a treasure which we
advertir secreto yerro tesoro
cannot easily acquire, nor sufficiently appreciate.
poder fácil adquirir suficiente apreciar

On JAMAS, NUNCA, NO, and MUY.†

What we do with pleasure we commonly‡ do very well.
gusto comun bien
Never [reproach] any one with the services which
echar en cara á servicio
thou doest to him. He who is a slave to his passions
esclavo
can never boast of being free. If a man cannot
vanagloriarse
find peace within his heart, he never will find it in
hallar dentro de
any other place. When they ask bishops if they
ninguno parte f. preguntar
wish to be bishops, they always answer, No. It is
querer siempre responder §
better to want riches, than ‖ to employ them badly.
carecer emplear mal
Men more easily forgive hatred than contempt. Never,
fácil perdonar odio desprecio

---

* See Grammar, p. 243.   † Ibid. p. 244.
‡ See Observation, Grammar, p. 244.   § Ibid.
‖ See Grammar, p. 245.

ON PREPOSITIONS. 109

no never, shall we see again those happy days! He is
               feliz
very angry, because his son is very much inclined to vice.
 enojado porque
You have offended her very much. When we last close
   ofender   *luego que finalmente*
our eyes our hopes [are at end] for ever and ever.
     acabarse

ON PREPOSITIONS.[*]

The unhappy minister lost all the hopes *on*
   desdichado *perder* *esperanza*
which his ambition had fed. And [taking out] *from*
       alimentarse   *sacar*
the pocket my ducats, I began to count them *within*
         comenzar contar
the hat. Heaven has united us again, *after* so many
sombrero el cielo   *juntar*
years *of* separation. All loved him; some *for* his gifts,
         querer   *dádiva*
others *for* his benevolence. We saw the valley *from* the
   benevolencia
top *of* the rock. Dame Jacinta was *by* my master.
cima   *Señora*   *amo*
Most times they punished me *without* reason. Every
    castigar
morning we rehearsed *after* the manner *of* players.
   ensayarse   *comediante*
He knew what he never had known *until* then. He was
saber
not elected *for* his erudition. This adventure did not
 elegir
seem to me the best omen *for* the rest of the journey.
parecer   *agüero*   *resto*   *viage*
Now then, asked the chapman coolly, How much
ahora bien preguntar *chalan frio* *quanto*
do you ask *for* your mule? *Before* his death he confessed
   pedir

[*] See Grammar, from p. 246 to 250.

the crime *before* several witnesses. Saying this, he drew
  delito   *testigo*   *decir*   *sacar*
from *under* the habit a leather purse. We had travelled
              cuero bolsa   *caminar*
above two miles. Their lamentations were mingled *with*
      milla   *lamento*   *mezclar*
the cries *of* the Indians. Trees are known *by* their
   grito   *Indio*
fruits. He saw himself compelled to place me *under*
              verse precisado poner
the rod *of* a preceptor. I placed *on* the table two
   férula ———   *mesa*
kinds *of* soup. Our Antipodes are not *beneath* us, nor
género   sopa   *antípoda*
we *beneath* them. He wrote *on* the nineteenth, that he
                              escribir
would set out *on* the twenty-second, but he was not
        partir   *estar*
back   *on* Friday. Let us humble ourselves *before*
de vuelta   *humillarse*
the Lord.

Rule 140. Prepositions govern the objective case; as,—*Me quexo de tí*, I complain of thee; *No puede vivir sin mí*, he cannot live without me.

Be always very much on [thy guard]. Cast thy eyes
estar   *sobre   tú*   *poner   ojo*
on me. How shall I be able to live without thee, after
en   yo   como   *poder vivir*   *tu*
having lived so long with thee? There was no
             tanto tiempo con
mercy   for me.
miséricordia

ON CONJUNCTIONS.

Rule 141. The conjunction *but*, not being preceded by a negative, is expressed by *pero* or *mas*; and after a negative it is construed *sino*; as,—I am rich, but I

ON CONJUNCTIONS. 111

am not happy, *yo soy rico, pero,* or *mas, no soy dichoso;* He is not happy, but rich, *no es dichoso, sino rico.*

Rule 142. The exceptive *but,* being preceded by an interrogative pronoun, or by a negative, is expressed by *sino;* and not following a negative is rendered *ménos;* as,—Who said it but you? *¿quien lo dixo sino vm.?* She eats nothing but fruit, *ella no come sino fruta;* She eats all but the rind, *ella come todo ménos la corteza.*

None *but* God can know our thoughts. She is con-
       conocer
tinually deceiving him, *but* nevertheless he likes her.
   engañar   *querer*
Every thing *but* the hour of death is uncertain. I do not complain of the law, *but* of her servants. Who caused
quexarse   *ministro* *hacer*
(2) humanity to (1) weep, *but* Nero? Death is terrible,
   A *llorar* *Neron*
but judgment will be more so: let us not fear then the
  juicio
hour of death, *but* the day of judgment. What his valour achieved was much, *but* what his mind suffered
obrar   *espíritu padecer*
was more. Fame is the reward of conquerors; *but*
   fama *recompensa conquistador*
virtue will have another recompense. Of what
       premio
[service was] to the Romans the death of Nero, *but* to
sirvió   *de*
make an opening for Otho and Vitellius? The happiness
dar A *entrada á Othon Vitelio* *dicha*
of a liberal and opulent man does not consist in having
dadivoso *rico*
riches, *but* in spending them, and not only in spending
    gastar

them, *but** in spending them well. We possess nothing
but perishable things.
poseer
perecedero

Note a.—But for thee my son would have been murdered. Without friendship the world would be *but*
asesinar
a wilderness. Why does he grieve? He (2) ought
desierto   *afligirse*   *deber*
(1) *rather* to rejoice at seeing himself among us. As he
alegrarse
lived, *so* he died. *Whether* thou be rich or poor, thou art not less obliged to be virtuous. He died on the
fallecer
twenty-fifth, *as* the clock struck three. We travelled
relox dar   *caminar*
without knowing *whether* it would be possible to arrive
saber   *llegar*
before day-break. I did not like his verse, *nor* his
amanecer   *gustar*   *verso*
prose *either.*
prosa

ON INTERJECTIONS.

Rule 143. Adjectives employed as interjections require *de* before the noun to which they are applied; as,—¡*Desdichada de mi madre!* Oh! my unhappy mother!

Unhappy we, how dreadful is war to those who
desdichado   *quan funesto*
undertake it! Happy thou, Telemachus! with such a
emprender
guide thou hast nothing to fear! Unhappy me! What shall I do? Whither shall I flee from my persecutors?
adonde   *huir*
Lo! they are here with us! Woe to those sinners who
ete†   ᴀ *aqui*   *ay*‡   *pecador*

* See note *a*, to Rule 141, Grammar.
† See note *b*.   ‡ See note *a*.

die in their sins! Woe to me, should death come
morir   *pecado*
before I am prepared!
        prevenido

ON COLLOQUIAL IDIOMS.

To act as, (*i. e.* in the capacity of,) *hacer de;* He acted as notary on that occasion, *hizo de escribano en aquella ocasion.*

To become, (*i. e* to be changed into,) *hacerse;* He became rich after the failure, *se hizo rico despues de la quiebra.*

To become, speaking of dress, is translated *caer* or *sentar;* Regimentals become him well, *el uniforme le cae,* or *le sienta bien.*

To become, in such expressions as the following, is translated *ser;* What will become of me! *¡que será de mi!*

To be in the right, *tener razon;* to be in the wrong, *no tener razon;* He is in the right to complain, *tiene razon de quexarse.*

To be near, or within an ace, is translated *estar á pique;* I was very near falling, *estuve á pique de caerme:* and sometimes by putting the second verb in the tense of the auxiliary, preceded by *por poco;* as, —*Por poco me caí.*

To be to, in such expressions as the following, is translated *ir;* The abdication was nothing to the subjects, *nada les iba á los vasallos en la abdicacion.*

To be to blame for, *tener la culpa de;* Am I then to blame for his cruelties? *¿Pues que tengo yo la culpa de sus crueldades?*

Both —— and, *Tanto —— como;* The king rewarded both the officers and soldiers, *el rey premió tanto á los oficiales como á los soldados.*

First Exercise on the foregoing Idioms.—In argument, he that is in the wrong generally talks loudest. She was
                                                              habla
very near losing her life. But for him, what would
              perder
have become of her! Señora Leonarda is in the right, said the old negro. Our footman acted as coachman in
decir   ——   *lacayo*   *cochero*
his absence. [As soon as] he becomes rich, he will
                  luego que
forget all his relations. Women generally prefer the
olvidarse   *pariente*   *preferir*
colours which are in fashion, although they may not
               de moda
become them so well as others. We were within an ace of being drowned. Both religion and virtue are the
      ahogarse   ——   *virtud*
bonds of civil society. What are his victories to the
vínculo —— *sociedad*
nation? He brought his niece home, in order that she
        traer   *sobrina*
might act as housekeeper. He acted as if the lives of
      ama de llaves   *obrar*
his soldiers were nothing to him, a cruelty for which the
 soldado   *crueldad*
soldiers themselves were to blame. Consider, man,
                               considerar
that when thou wilt be very near dying, it will not
    quando
then be a time to think on what will become of thee!
entónces   *pensar*

To care, in such expressions as the following, is translated *darse*; I care nothing for his threats, *nada se me da de sus amenazas.*

To fancy, (whimsically,) *antojarse á;* They fancied

that all would applaud them, *se les antojó que todos los aplaudirian;* She fancied apples, *se le antojaron manzanas.*

To give blessings, *echar bendiciones;* Give them thy blessing, *échales tu bendicion.*

To have to do, in such expressions as the following, is translated *tener que ver;* What have the conquests of the Carthaginians to do with what I say? *¿Que tienen que ver las conquistas de los Cartagineses con lo que yo digo?*

To have weight with, *hacer fuerza á;* All that he said had no weight with the minister, *todo lo que dixo no le hizo ninguna fuerza al ministro.*

However, in such expressions as the following, is translated *por;* However great may be his merit, *por grande que sea su mérito.*

To lay the blame on, *echar la culpa á;* All the nation laid the blame on ministers, *toda la nacion echó la culpa á los ministros.*

To look, in speaking of inanimate objects, *caer;* My windows looked to the garden, *mis ventanas caian al jardin.*

Second Exercise.—However good and wise a king may be, still he is a man. And if the boy [turns out]
               aun   *salir*
mischievous, every one will lay the blame on thee.
travieso
As his victories would have been nothing to his subjects, what did they care whether he conquered or
vasallo   *vencer ó*
was conquered? When men are prejudiced, there is no
                           preocupado
argument that has any weight with them. The front
argumento   *fachada*

of the church looked towards the East. What had his
oriente
former victories to do with that defeat? He told me
antiguo   *derrota*   *decir*
that he envied my husband's lot, however unfortunate
envidia   *suerte* f.   *desgraciado*
it might be. And after having given them his blessing, he
closed his eyes for ever. Men often lay the blame on their
cerrar
ill luck, when only their ill conduct is to blame. Some
conducta
women fancy that every one that [looks at] them is [in love]
mirar   *enamorado*
with them. Children fancy every thing they see. How-
de   *niño*   *ver*
ever scarce true love may be, it is even less scarce than
raro   *aun*
true friendship.
amistad

To make pay, in such expressions as the following, is translated *llevar á;* They made my father pay a thousand pounds for the farm, *le llevaron á mi padre mil libras por el cortijo.*

To make up one's mind, *consentir en;* The innkeeper had made up his mind to gain a great deal on this occasion, *el mesonero habia consentido en ganar mucho en esta ocasion.*

To miss, (*i. e.* to feel a loss,) *echar menos;* As soon as I put my hand into my pocket, I missed my purse, *luego que metí la mano en la faltriquera eché menos mi bolsa.*

To pay attention to, *hacer caso de;* He pays no attention to what I say, *no hace caso de lo que digo.*

To serve for, (*i. e.* in place of,) *servir de;* A stone served him for a pillow, *una piedra le servia de almohada.*

ON COLLOQUIAL IDIOMS.

To smell of, or like, *oler á;* His clothes smell still of gunpowder, *aun huelen sus vestidos á pólvora.*

To spare, (*i. e.* to omit,) *perdonar;* He spared no diligence, *no perdonó diligencia alguna.*

To spoil, *echar á perder;* He spoils every thing he does, *echa á perder todo lo que hace.*

To stand in, (*i. e.* to cost,) *salir á;* This work stood the proprietor in two guineas a volume, *esta obra le salió al propietario á dos guineas el tomo.* When the value, and not the rate, is mentioned, it is translated *tener de costa;* It stood the proprietor in a hundred pounds, *le tuvo al propietario cien libras de costa.*

Third Exercise.—What I can assure thee is, that I shall spare no opportunity of mocking thy vigilance.
        ocasion *burlar* *vigilancia*
Sometimes we will amuse ourselves with hunting,
            en *
at others with fishing, and so I hope that you will
  en *   *esperar*
not miss the city. I took him for the gardener, and
    ciudad *tener*   *jardinero*
for [that time] I paid no attention to him. And from
por entónces   *desde*
[that moment] I made up my mind, that I should not
 luego
spend the time badly in the country. Wash this bottle;
pasar *mal*   *lavar*
it smells of vinegar. The salt water had spoiled all
   vinagre *salado*
the powder. This pipe stands him in a hundred pounds,
 pólvora *pipa*
and the wine he drank before used to stand me in
      beber

* See note *b* to Rule 136, Grammar.

seven shillings a bottle. From [that time] caves
entónces   soterraneo
served for an asylum to people of our profession. We
asilo   gente f.   *profesion*
shall not make them pay to-day as much as they made
hoy
her pay yesterday. When a man loses his liberty he
ayer   perder
serves as an instrument to enslave others.
esclavizar

To take one's fancy, *caer en gracia á*; He used to make us repeat all the airs which took her fancy, *él nos hacia repetir todas las tonadillas que le cáian á ella en gracia*.

To take amiss, *llevar á mal*; He did not take amiss what I said, *no llevó á mal lo que dixe*.

To take for granted, *dar por supuesto*; I take it for granted that you won't come with me, *doy por supuesto que vm. no quiere venir conmigo*.

To taste of, or like, *saber á*; This wine tastes like vinegar, *este vino sabe á vinagre*.

To think, preceded by the adverb *rather*, or by *to be inclined*, is translated *estar en*, in such expressions as the following; I rather think that he won't come to-day, *estoy en que no vendrá hoy*.

To try, (*i. e.* to endeavour,) *hacer por*; I shall try to come, *haré por venir*.

To wonder, (*i. e.* to be at a loss to know,) is not translated, and the verb governed is put in one of the futures of the indicative, or in the imperfect of the subjunctive, preceded by the conjunction *si*; I wonder whether these complaints will ever end? *¿Si se acabarán jamas estas quexas?* I wonder whether the enemy's loss has been great? ¿Si habrá sido grande la pérdida del enemigo?

Fourth Exercise.—I took for granted that I was going to lose my life with my poor ducats. It is said
   ir   *perder*   *ducado*
that the manna, which fell in the desert, tasted of that
   maná   *caer*   *desierto*
which each one of the Israelites liked most. Some men
   Israelita gustar
die bachelors, because no woman takes their fancy, and
soltero
others, because they have not taken any woman's fancy. He never thought she would have taken amiss his pro-
   pensar   *pro-*
posal. I wonder whether he will accept the conditions.
puesta   *aceptar*
I rather think he [will not be contented] with what they
   contentarse
offer him. Had he tried to comfort her, her affliction
ofrecer   *consolar*   *afliccion*
would have been less. I am inclined to think that he will take it for granted that we shall not consent to it. They presented me to the duke, and I had the
   presentar   *duque*
[good fortune] of taking his fancy.
   dicha

ON SYNONYMS.*

Adonde, Donde.—Page 11.

Exercise.—Every one related whither he was going.
   contar
They repaired whither the negro and I were. I accom-
   acudir   ———   *acom-*
panied her to her house, where a grand-daughter of hers
pañar   *nieta*
was indisposed. I don't like to go whither you say, be-
indispuesta   *querer*

* See Synonyms of the Spanish Language, by the Author.

cause I like better to stay where I am. [Be not eager]
  gustar   *quedarse*   *apresurarse*
to heap up riches; because where thy treasure is, thy
amontonar
heart will be also. In vain the murderer endeavours to
          asesino *esforzarse*
conceal himself where he can; whither shall he go, that
ocultarse
the voice of conscience may not reach him?
           alcanzar

Agarrar, Asir.—Page 129.

Exercise.—And the wife of Potiphar seized him by the
        Putifar
border of his garment, but he left her his mantle and fled.
orla *vestidura*   *manto* *huir*
I took hold of his arm, and we retired to a coffee-house.
    brazo   *retirarse*   *café*
He seized the tree with both hands, and pulled it
   árbol   *mano* f. *arrancar*
up. He seized the delinquent by the arm, and conducted
á   *delingüente*   *conducir*
him to the presence of the judge. Had I not seized the
  presencia
rope that they threw me, I should have been drowned.
soga *echar*   *ahogarse*
Had they seized him by the arm, instead of laying hold of
         en lugar
him by the coat epaulette, he would not have escaped.
 casaca charretera   *escaparse*

Ahí, Allí, Allá.—Page 122.
Aquí, Acá.—Page 123.

Exercise.—Here we are to sleep. Neither gold nor
    dormir
silver was seen there. Come hither. Here thou wilt
    ver   *venir*
live in peace. Not only the culprit, but his accusers
vivir *paz*   *reo*   *acusador*

were likewise there. Take him to prison, said the
    tambien   *llevar*   *la cárcel*
judge, there let him learn to obey: immediately they
                aprender
[laid hands on] the delinquent, and conducted him
echaron mano a   *conducir*
thither. I wish to see the wound you have there. He
        querer   *herida*
told me, that, as he was coming hither one night, an
decir   *venir*
assassin wounded him in the breast; and to convince me,
asesino *herir*   *pecho*   *convencer*
he showed me the scar he had there. You write
   mostrar   *cicatriz* f.   *vm. escribir*
from France, that you do not wish to stay there:
                      querer *quedarse*
remember that you might have remained here, but
acordarse   *permanecer*
went thither against my consent: as you cannot return
ir   *voluntad*   *volver*
hither, if you like Italy, you may go thither, and try to
        gustar
establish yourself there.

Debe, Debe de.—Page 138.

Exercise.—The conditions ought to be advantageous,
otherwise they will not be accepted. We must be
de otro modo
merciful. Pride must be his predominant passion, else
                   dominante   *sino*
he would not have done it. I say that she must be merciful, because she forgave him. He must repent, if he
    pues   *perdonar*   *arrepentirse*
wishes to be pardoned. To spend as much as he does,
querer   *gastar*
a man ought to be rich; but [according to] what is said
                          segun
of that gentleman, he must be very poor.

122 ON SYNONYMS.

Ser preciso, Ser menester.—Page 115.

Exercise.—It is necessary to die, and we must bear
                          morir   *llevar*
death with resignation. It is necessary that we should
bear with patience the troubles of this life. The cook,
                     trabajo   *cocinera*
for it is necessary that I should describe her, was a
porque   *describir*
person of sixty years. To be saved it is necessary to
                                  salvar
be virtuous. You must wrap yourself well up, in that
   virtuoso   *abrigarse*
climate. To soften wax, it is necessary to warm it.
clima m.   *ablandar cera*   *calentar*

Honor, Honra.—Page 153.

Exercise.—He was buried in the Chapel Royal, an
              enterrar   *Capilla Real*
honour which he well deserved. Let us act always as men
                   merecer   *obrar*
of honour. Honour ought never to be sacrificed. The
duke did me the honour of appointing me his secretary.
                                nombrar
The pomp of funerals regards more the vanity of the
   pompa   *entierro*   *mirar*
living, than the honour of the dead.
vivo   *muerto*

Lograr, Conseguir, Alcanzar.—Page 172.

Exercise.—How shall I be able [to get out] of this
            como   *salir*
prison, when they have just taken from me the means
                          quitar   *medio*
of obtaining it? You will be able to support yourself
                            poder   *mantener*
with the money until you obtain some employment.
               hasta que
So capricious is fortune, that those who do not seek her
                                      buscar

obtain her greatest favours. The frogs besought Jupiter
                                       rana suplicar
so much, that [at length] they obtained a king. Had he
                al fin
not received reinforcements, he never would have obtained the victory.

Luego, Despues.—Page 165.

Exercise.—After I satisfied his curiosity, [Well now,]
                        satisfacer   *ahora bien*
Gil Blas, said he to me. But after they understood the
                                              entender
origin of the noise, their uneasiness [was changed] into
                              inquietud convertirse en
loud   peals   of laughter. After the captain of
grande carcaxada
robbers had made this apology, he got into bed.
vandolero   *meterse*
After they expelled their enemies, they returned to their cities. After the sun appears, all bodies cast a shadow.
                        salir   *hacer* A

No obstante, Aunque, Bienque.—Page 162.

Exercise.—They have lost the battle, though, considering
                                  perder
the enemy's superiority, it is not to be wondered at. It rains, though the wind is changed. The emperor and the prince are both great generals, though the latter is certainly very superior. She would not marry him, though
                                                      asarse
he were rich. The atheist denies the existence of God, although
              ateista negar   existencia
all the works of nature proclaim his omnipotence.
        obra   declarar   omnipotencia

Opinion, Parecer, Dictamen.—Page 177.

Exercise.—Physicians do not always declare their opinion.
                médico
According to the opinion of the surgeon, the
                                    cirujano

g 2

wound is not mortal. Many find themselves compelled
herida   *verse   precisado*
to act against their own opinion. The good man replied,
                                   bueno hombre
I am not of thy uncle's opinion. He always abides
              tio   *arreglarse*
by the opinion of his physician. Ptolemy was of opinion
                                 Ptolemo
that the sun revolved round the earth.
         revolver

Pertenecer, Corresponder.—Page 171.

Exercise.—This house belonged to the hospital for
many years. The title of majesty belongs to kings.
               tratamiento
According to her father's will the estate belongs
                         testamento hacienda
to the widow, but it has been divided among all. That
    viuda   *repartir*
colony has always belonged to the Dutch. Having
colonia
divided the conquered kingdoms into several portions,
each belligerent power took that which belonged to it.
        potencia

Porque, Pues.—Page 169.

Exercise.—He demanded of me my daughter, because
             pedir
she is pretty; and I refused her to him, because he is
   bonito   *negar*
ugly; he will find another wife, because he is rich; and
feo   *hallar*
will repent, because he is old; he will forget my
   arrepentirse   *olvidar*
daughter, because he does not love her, and will not
   ruin me, because I am so already. And thus my
arruinar   *ya*

ON SYNONYMS. 125

master lost his life, because his physician did not know
médico
Greek. He will obtain the situation, without doubt,
el Griego   *puesto*
because he has good friends.

Sospecha, Rezelo.—Page 130.

Exercise.—They had not any suspicion of the trick I
pieza
had played them. We suspected that they were coming to take us. I had some suspicions that he loved another
prender
woman more than me. We always suspected that he would leave us a good legacy. Not to render myself
    dexar   *hacerse*
suspicious, I did not frequent the house.

Veneno, Ponzoña.—Page 160.

Exercise.—There are snakes in the island of Ceylon,
culebra   *isla*   *Ceylan*
whose poison kills in four hours. He suspected that
matar
there was some poison in his drink. The poison of these
bebida
insects is in the sting. Each poison has its antidote.
insecto   *aguijon*   *antidoto*
Poisons belong to the animal, vegetable, and mineral
———— *vegetal* ————
kingdoms.

Para, Por.—See page 1.

To write well [we must] have good pens, good ink,
ser preciso
and good paper. Willingly would I go so far to hear
de buena gana
him; but to hear him well you must be seated close to
cerca
him. The frog stretched herself so much to [be equal]
       rana   *igualar*

to the ox, that at length she burst. All men are born
                rebentar   *nacer*
to die, and to die well we must live well.
                           vivir

Alguien, Alguno, Nadie, Ninguno.—Pages 28, 29.

No one but God can know our thoughts. Is there
                      pensamiento
any one who can tell what his end will be? Among all
                                       entre
the authors which I have examined, I found none that
                    exáminar   *encontrar*
makes mention of the event. He exclaimed thrice, is
                                  lance
there any one within? but no one answered, because
none of them wished to be discovered. The captain,
                         descubrir
having exhorted his soldiers to follow him, marched
      exhortar   *seguir*
valiantly towards the fortress, but no one stirred.
                                          moverse

Abajo, Bajo, Debajo.—Page 5.

Send her the letter under cover. Whose are the
                          cubierta
books that are under the table? The title is written
                        mesa
at the top and the date at the bottom. [Seeing himself]
                 fecha   *verse*
compelled to place me under the rod of a preceptor,
precisado   *poner*   *férula*
he sent me to Doctor Godinez. The different aspects
enviar
under which good and evil [present themselves] to us,
                                       presentarse
occasion our instability in what we desire.
causar

Aun, Todavia.—Page 12.

We have received the [bills of lading], but the ship is
conocimiento *navio*
not yet arrived. I would sacrifice my fortune, and even
caudal
my life for her. I am waiting for them yet. I sprained
torcer
my foot yesterday, and I feel the pain yet. We are still
sentir
without letters. I told you to give her the money,
entregar
and you have not given it to her yet.

Prevenir, Advertir.—Page 75.

You permit them to return as late as they like, with-
volver *tarde* *querer*
out noticing it to them. Had you warned your friend of
the danger, he would not have embarked. The king
peligro *embarcarse*
warned his ministers not to mention the subject to him
ministro *asunto*
again. Warn your servant not to come here again. The
criado
general wrote to the emperor, representing to him the
escribir
services of the captain who was the bearer of the
portador
dispatches.

Agradar, Gustar.—Page 50.

Exercise.—The congregation liked the sermon, but did
auditorio *sermon*
not like the preacher's voice. Who can like a conduct
predicador *voz*
dictated by such interested motives? I never liked his
dictar *interesado*
similes. Would you like a shepherd's life? However
pastor

relishing may be the draughts which physicians prescribe
sabroso   *bebida·*   *médico·*   *recetar*
few are the patients that like them. All men like to
               enfermo
hear themselves praised, but none likes to hear his con-
              alabar
duct censured. We must abandon all our earthly
    censurar   *abandonar*   *terrestre*
enjoyments, whether we like it or do not like it.

Voz, Palabra.—Page 167.

Exercise.—His style is full of high-sounding words.
                       altisonante
We have had some words with them. He concluded his
                          concluir
letter with these words. The word *ennui* is a French
carta
word, and a word very difficult to pronounce. He re-
            difícil   *re-*
peated it word by word. All my words had no weight
petir
with her. Many words in that language have no plural.
                       idioma
He answered not a word. These words are offensive to
                           ofensivo
modesty. Avoid cutting words. His writings abound in
pudor   *picante*
foreign words. Never give your word without having
first considered whether you can keep it.
       poder cumplir

THE END.